WONDERLURE

WONDERLURE

BEING LURED INTO THE WONDER OF GOD'S PRESENCE

JASON LAWSON

AMBASSADOR INTERNATIONAL
GREENVILLE, SOUTH CAROLINA & BELFAST, NORTHERN IRELAND
www.ambassador-international.com

WONDERLURE
BEING LURED INTO THE WONDER OF GOD'S PRESENCE
©2025 by Jason Lawson
All rights reserved

ISBN: 978-1-64960-733-1, hardcover
ISBN: 978-1-64960-632-7, paperback
eISBN: 978-1-64960-681-5

Cover Design and Interior Typesetting by Karen Slayne
Edited by Megan Griffin

No part of this publication may be reproduced, distributed, or transmitted in any form or by any means, including photocopying, recording, or other electronic or mechanical methods, without the prior written permission of the publisher, except in the case of brief quotations embodied in critical reviews and certain other noncommercial uses permitted by copyright law. For permission requests, contact the publisher using the information below.

Scripture quotations taken from the (NASB®) New American Standard Bible®, Copyright © 1960, 1971, 1977, 1995 by The Lockman Foundation. Used by permission. All rights reserved. lockman.org

Ambassador International titles may be purchased in bulk for education, business, fundraising, or sales promotional use. For information, please email sales@emeraldhouse.com.

AMBASSADOR INTERNATIONAL
Emerald House
411 University Ridge, Suite B14
Greenville, SC 29601
United States
www.ambassador-international.com

AMBASSADOR BOOKS
The Mount
2 Woodstock Link
Belfast, BT6 8DD
Northern Ireland, United Kingdom
www.ambassadormedia.co.uk

The colophon is a trademark of Ambassador, a Christian publishing company.

Special Thanks

Thank you, Mom and Dad, for teaching me from a young age to know the wonder of God's presence.

ENDORSEMENTS

"*Wonderlure* truly fulfills its purpose of luring us to desire God's presence above all else."

—**Bev Dawson**
Missionary to the Wapishana people of Guyana

"I started reading *Wonderlure* thinking I was going to read a little easy-to-read book on the wonder of walking with God. I finished feeling grateful to have walked through Jason's journey through these pages and inspired to continue to be lured into God's presence."

—**Brenda Gray**
Executive Vice President
Development and Communications of
Baptist Children's Home of North Carolina

"*Wonderlure* illuminates the path to walking with God in such a way that it impacts each step you take as you become more like Christ."

—**Louis Chaney**
Ministry Director, Greensboro Youth For Christ

ENDORSEMENTS
(cont.)

"Jason has one of the most creative, childlike, and pastoral hearts of anyone I know. I have been blessed and inspired by his earnest pursuit of the Father."

—**Seth Williams**
CEO, The Inn of Last Resort

"This is not just a must-read book but a must-do book, not of works, but of agreement and hope."

—**Renee Leonard Kennedy**
Author, *After the Flowers Die*
Co-host, *The Moral Tea* Podcast

CONTENTS

3
Preface

CHAPTER ONE 7
Walking with Emmanuel

CHAPTER TWO 25
Following the Lamb

CHAPTER THREE 37
Abiding on the Vine

CHAPTER FOUR 53
Aligning with the Cornerstone

CHAPTER FIVE 69
Knowing the Father

CHAPTER SIX 81
Watching for Messiah

CHAPTER SIX 91
Trusting the Sunrise from on High

103
Wonderlure

PREFACE

I had a dream that my family and I were raptured. We stood in the midst of a huge number of people outside Heaven's gates. No one rushed, pushed, or got irritated. Together, we laughed, cried, and hugged. My daughter was there, even though she had not been born yet. I cannot describe to you what it was like to overflow with the joy of Heaven. When it was my time to enter through the gate, I walked in; and there before me was the Father seated on His throne, Jesus standing at His right hand, and the Spirit of God hovering on His left. I embraced the Son, bowed before the Father, and talked with the Spirit before moving on into Heaven. Once I was rejoined with my family, we walked the golden streets. I do not know if the streets were actually made of gold; but they reflected the golden light, which came from the top of a large, grassy hill on our right. There was a dirt path that wound its way up to the top of the hill. You could tell this was a path that had been walked many times.

My sons and I began to run around the base of the hill when, all of a sudden, we found that we were lifting up off the ground. We flew through the air playing tag and laughing. Finally, we were joined in the air by my wife with our daughter in her arms. We had been forever changed.

After landing back on the ground, we started racing up the dirt path. While people were walking around, some were carrying things like bags or baskets; but no one seemed to be weighed down by the burden of their package. I stopped to talk to a man who had a sack on his back. I asked him why he didn't just fly up to the top of the hill instead of walking the whole way. His response to this day draws me in. "If you are in the presence of God, what does it matter rather you walk, run, or soar?"

I woke up shortly after that; and while I have dreamed several times of going back to Heaven, I have never made it to the top of that grassy hill. But I have also never forgotten those words.

What would it be like if we walked with God? What would it matter if we walked, ran, or soared? I can only imagine when you walk with God as Enoch did in Genesis 5:24, your perspective would change. What once was now seems to be nothing more than dust, and what wasn't now appears to be greater than all the wealth of the world. God's presence has a way of changing you. The wonder of His glory has a way of opening your eyes so you can see things rightly. You are altered; you are refreshed; you are changed and renewed. No one can understand this unless they, too, have walked with God.

And isn't that what the Father wants more than anything? He is not just asking you to come to Him, nor is He begging. No, He lures you with His wonder; and when you enter in, life becomes alive. So much so, I had to create a word because nothing else could express it. *Wonderlure*—being lured into the wonder of God's presence. Are you ready to start a journey that could change you forever? Are you ready to take the bait God has set before you? One step at a time, one moment, one breath, one glance can make all the difference because we are now on His holy ground.

Leave behind the things you understand and allow God to take you on a tour of what you don't know. He leads, so be listening for His voice and watch carefully in case He changes directions. Let nothing deter you from walking in step with Him. Believe me, the enemy will do everything he can to distract you and throw off your foot. If you fall, get back up and ask the Father to point you in the right direction. You must desire His presence more than any earthly thing. You must be lured into the wonder of God's glory. I hope you enjoy this *wonderlure*!

Jason Lawson

WALKING WITH EMMANUEL

"The Patron Saint of Worms"

A simple creature of foolish mind,
Started a journey undone.
Now caught partway by the morning sun,
He's doomed to dry in the sun.
I watched it wither; I watched it writhe.
For what did it matter to me?
This creature is small and too far gone,
The like, too many to see.
Why should I waste my time with meager worms,
Their imminent death at hand?
But my heart ached, and my soul was moved
Because I, too, was a worm of a man.

—Jason Lawson

> *"What is man that You take thought of him,*
> *And a son of man that You care for him?"*
>
> —PSALM 8:4

Walking With God

What does it mean to "walk with God"? Is this some theological metaphor for the Christian life, or is it a mystical journey where God comes down to interact with us? I will leave the outcome of what that means to you and God. But that's just the point. God can speak for Himself. Either God is alive, or He is not. Either God is personal, or He is not. Either God is able, or He is not. You are free to do as you wish with your understanding of God; but for me, if Jesus says that He was leaving to prepare a place for us and would be returning, then I believe He is coming back. And if He says that the Father is sending His Holy Spirit to be with us until He returns, then I believe the Spirit of God is among us. And if the Spirit of God is busy confirming, convicting, teaching, and comforting us, then I believe His work effects our day to day lives. I trust He will teach you what it means to walk with God. Our journey begins with listening and watching for God to direct us in our day-to-day and even moment-to-moment lives.

God's Yoke

For me, my journey of wanting to walk with God came after preaching on Matthew 11:28-30: "'Come to Me, all who are weary and heavy-laden, and I will give you rest. Take My yoke upon you and learn from Me, for I am gentle and humble in heart, and you will find rest for your souls. For My yoke is easy and My burden is light.'" The part that really got me was, "'Take My yoke upon you and learn from Me.'" I began trying to really think on this so I could rightly teach this passage. I knew a yoke was a tool used to harness oxen together, so they could plow in tandem with greater strength than if they plowed on their own. But what did it mean to put God's yoke on me? Did that mean God was on one side of that yoke and I was on the other? Or did it mean that I was on one side and fellow Christians were on the other side, while God was the farmer directing us? After working and studying this passage, I ended up teaching it from both perspectives. But I was fascinated by the thought that God might be pulling next to me.

When farmers plowed with oxen, they would try to have equally strong oxen pulling so that one would not over pull the other which would result in a crooked furrow running across the field. But at times, the farmer would put a more experienced ox on one side and a less-experienced ox on the other; so the more mature ox would train the other one. This is most certainly the case if God and I are in this yoke together. But we can't miss the second part of this phrase: "and learn from Me." What has God taught you lately? I'm not talking about what has your pastor taught you nor the author of the devotional you are reading. What has God taught you personally? Believe me, when God does the teaching, there's going to be some learning.

Pulling, Tugging, and Walking

Here are three quick lessons I have learned when pulling in tandem with God. First, there are times when I get so excited about an idea, I shoot out the gate so fast, my dust doesn't settle for weeks.

The Bible tells us to "serve the Lord with gladness" (Psalm 100:2); but in these moments, I find myself serving the Lord with zeal. When I fall asleep, I'm thinking about an idea;, and when I wake up, it's the first thing on my mind. I find myself so stressed. My heart is beating out of my chest. My head is spinning, and my eyes feel like they're going to pop out of their sockets. These are the undeniable signs that God is working and Satan is fighting, right? No, stress is not righteous, nor is it sinful. Stress is simply how we cope with what's going on around us. What we do with stress can be righteous or sinful; but in itself, stress is just an indicator. When I am wearing God's yoke and pulling in tandem with Him, stress can be a really good indicator that I'm pulling ahead of God. It's what happens when I use all my energy and strength to pull God along. I will not win this tug-of-war. Instead, I should use stress as a warning light. When I'm running full tilt but filling stressed, then I need to assess whether or not I'm running ahead of God. In these moments, I need to repent and ask God to slow down my zeal so that I can walk with Him.

The second lesson I have learned is that we sometimes find ourselves in a season of rest while walking yoked with God. God leads us to green grass and still water. Rest after a season of storms is a wonderful thing. But if we are not careful, that season of rest can become a life of denial. We begin to worship our comfort, but that is okay because we are living in God's rest, right? While it is true that God graciously gives us seasons of rest, it is also true that we can sometimes get so comfortable in that rest that we become complacent. Life flies by while we just wait for death to take us out, and astoundingly, we are good with this. Sadly, what has happened is we remained content to lie in our state of rest even after God got up and started pressing forward. We lazily sat in the green grass until the weeds overtook us. Now our spiritual muscles have atrophied to the point it's going to hurt when we try to stand again. Not all stress or pain in life are signs that Satan is fighting us. Sometimes, they are signs that God is prodding us.

Finally, the third lesson God taught me from Matthew 11:28-30 is when I walk yoked together with God, then the strength we pull with is far more powerful than I could muster alone. I begin to learn to work in the strength of the LORD. He leads me in the direction I should go, how fast I should pull, when to rest, and when to get back at it. Everything He has called me to do is wrapped up in walking with Him.

Would you say you tend to get ahead of God, fall behind Him, or walk in step with Him? How has this effected your life?

_____

_____

_____

_____

_____

Walking Alongside God

Let's break down a little further what it means to walk with Emmanuel. Some time ago, God led me to a verse that utterly changed my life. It is a small verse found in a book of the Bible many people do not even know exists. Amos 3:3 says, "Do two men walk together unless they have made an appointment?" The word "appointment" can also mean "agreement." When we think about this, it is not possible for two people to walk together unless they have agreed on a few things.

The Agreement of Person

If I walked into a room full of people and said, "Would you like to go for a walk?" then it would be possible that everyone would follow me on my walk or only some people would. There has to be an understanding of who you are inviting to walk with you. In terms of walking with God, who are you asking? First off, it is vitally important that you understand that God is not your homeboy or your bestie or "the Man upstairs." Those who have a view of God with such a limited scope are sure to be walking alone. Isaiah 7:14 states, "Therefore the Lord Himself will give you a sign: Behold, a virgin will be with child and bear a son, and she will call His name Immanuel." Immanuel—or Emmanuel—means, "God with us." God—the Creator, Ruler, Sustainer, and Savior of the world—has come to be with us. If you want a peak into the Person and responsibilities of God, then go read Job 38-41. When you can respond to God better than Job did, then you can call Him some term of equality. But until you can match His limitless grandeur, you had better refer to Him with fear and honor.

We cannot stop here. We must dig deeper into God's character and what that means for us to walk with Him. Again, if we are to learn more, we must look in another obscure passage of Scripture. Deuteronomy 23:14 says, "Since the LORD your God walks in the midst of your camp to deliver you and to defeat your enemies before you, therefore your camp must be holy; and He must not see anything indecent among you or He will turn away from you." A few things that we can draw out of the verse are the character of God, a truth about God, and a truth about us.

First, we can see that one of the descriptions of God's character is that He is holy. This means that He is set apart from anything that is not like Him. God is perfectly right with nothing wrong, broken, or compromised. If something that is clean comes in contact with something dirty, then it ceases to be clean. Think of it this way: on Sunday morning, a parent will go through great pains to get their daughter clean and dressed for church. Once she is sufficiently attired in her bright white dress, then her parents will threaten her within an inch of her life if she gets close to even a speck of dirt. In the mind of the child, dirt and the chocolate cake that was made for Sunday dinner are very different. So when the parent walks back into the kitchen to discover their clean, beautiful offspring is now covered head to toe in chocolate ganache, they are bewildered as to what went wrong.

God, on the other hand, is not subject to splitting hairs or rationalizing the possibilities of toying with the line we call sin. God is perfectly right, and He will not be in the presence of sin or sinful things. If you desire to walk with Emmanuel, then understand that God does not play the games we so often play with the world. "You adulteresses, do you not know that friendship with the world is hostility toward God? Therefore whoever wishes to be a friend of the world makes himself an enemy of God" (James 4:4). God sent His only Son to die on a cross to wash away the filth of our sin. He does not find our movies entertaining, nor does He think our dirty jokes are funny. These worldly pleasures cost Him very deeply. He sees them as adultery to our covenant relationship. They are the very things that brought pain and death to His Son, and He will not tolerate being in the same space as them. No, God is holy and perfectly right, and He will not be contaminated by our trash. This means that if we allow the sins of this world to consume us, we will never be holy like God. Although we can never perfectly match up to God's holiness, He calls us to live holy lives because He is holy.

Next, we are given the truth that God walks among us. God is not just a Divine Being Who watches us from somewhere up in Heaven. He is a Divine Being in Heaven Who also walks *with* each and every one of us. Emmanuel cannot stop being *with* us, or else He ceases to be Emmanuel. During Bible times, His presence with us existed in the form of Jesus Christ, Who physically walked the earth with His disciples. Once Jesus returned to Heaven, the Holy Spirit came to live in the hearts of believers. This is how He exists with us in the present day until Jesus returns once again. Holy Emmanuel, Who is perfectly right, walks among us; but He will not stay among our disrespectful filth.

Finally, there is an important truth that we as God's desired creations need to understand. God wants us to walk through life with Him, but there is a specific way for this to happen. Micah 6:8 says, "He has told you, O man, what is good; And what does the Lord require of you But to do justice, to love kindness, And to walk humbly with your God?" We do not get to walk with God unless it is God with Whom we walk. I mean that life changes when God reveals Himself to us. I'm not talking about a Bible story from Sunday school nor an object lesson from a book. I'm talking about God Himself meeting you while you are hopelessly lost and showing you that He has transferred your death to His Son's life. We are backstabbing, thieving adulteresses, yet He still clothes us in His righteousness and clothes Himself in our iniquity. How could we ever disrespectfully refer to our Savior in terms that are anything other than worship? Micah tells us, if we are to walk with God, then it should be humbly with a right view of who He is.

In light of Amos 3:3 and the agreement we must have to walk with Him, it starts with you knowing Who He is. God is not like us, and we are not like Him. He is far greater than anything we can imagine; therefore, His sacrifice of becoming Emmanuel means far more than we can comprehend.

The Agreement of Path

If you are to walk alongside God, then you must know Who He is; but you must also understand the path He walks. David prays this to God in Psalm 27:11: "Teach me Your way, O Lord, And lead me in a level path Because of my foes." God does have a path which He walks, and David is asking to walk with Him. The path Emmanuel walks has several names. Jeremiah calls it the "ancient paths" (Jer. 6:16). David calls it the "blameless way" (Psalm 101:2). He also called it the "paths of righteousness" (Psalm 23:3). Paul called it the "path of peace" (Rom. 3:17). It is plain to see that the path Emmanuel walks is not a path that humanity frequents. There is a reason for that. The path Emmanuel walks on is one of discipline. It is narrow, and few find it (Matt. 7:14). Then once you have found the path, it is easy to lose your way. Proverb 4:25-27 says, "Let your eyes look directly ahead And let your gaze be fixed straight in front of you. Watch the path of your feet And all your ways will be established. Do not turn to the right nor to the left; Turn your foot from evil." We live in a world full of distractions. Our adversary loves nothing more than to get us to look to the right or the left, and we are so quick to get distracted by the things of the world. We follow Satan's bait right off the path God walks; and then when we come to our senses, we have become so tangled in the briars of this life that we become disheartened. No, walking the "ancient paths" or the "path of peace" is not easy. It is a discipline that we must learn. Praise God, Emmanuel longs to teach us this as we walk His paths together.

Now before we get too keyed up about walking the paths of righteousness together, it would be good to note a couple of verses that give us some previews as to what we might be looking for. If we think walking with Emmanuel will be a gentle stroll alongside the wildflowers in the green meadow while the golden sun warms us and our hearts with inexplicable joy and peace, then we had better go back to His Word. Nahum 1:3 tells us, "The LORD is slow to anger and great in power, And the LORD will by no means leave *the guilty* unpunished. In whirlwind and storm is His way, And clouds are the dust beneath His feet."

How does that sound to you? God's ways are in the whirlwind and the storm. Most people will live their lives running from the whirlwinds. Whirlwinds have a way of birthing chaos in our lives. They are a gateway to death and destruction. It's fascinating where in Scripture a whirlwind will pop up. Job 38:1 says, "Then the LORD answered Job out of the whirlwind and said, 'What! Does this mean that while Job's friends are accusing him of sin, some whirlwind in the corner just starts talking to him? No, God, in the whirlwind, began speaking to him. It is not easy to stay in the presence of whirlwinds. They scare us, and we worry about what could happen if they stay around too long; but God's ways are in the whirlwind. It is important to note that the whirlwind is not God, but rather it is God in the whirlwind. A whirlwind is the same today as it was thousands of years ago: chaos, war, loss of loved ones, eviction notices, being let go from a job, bad diagnosis, overdue bills, etc. These things are not God, but He is in these whirlwind moments. He walks in the midst of them because we walk in the midst of them. Don't run from them; run to God, Who is in those whirlwind moments, and ask Him to reveal Himself to you.

God's ways are also in the storms. In the Gospels when the disciples are in the boat and the storm comes up, they all freaked out. They cried out in fear because storms have a way of rocking the boat. They disrupt what was supposed to be a pleasant experience. But Jesus was not bothered by the storm. In fact, He found the storm to be a great place to take a nap. Are you ready to walk the stormy paths of Emmanuel?

Nahum tells us, "Clouds are the dust beneath His feet." Clouds block the light. When clouds roll in, they can deceive us into believing that the sun is not shining. In reality, the sun is shining brightly above the clouds. But below, we can find ourselves struggling with seasonal depression on cloudy days. Clouds can also lower themselves and envelop us in their fog. It is easy to become confused in the fog and fear we will lose our way. But Scripture tells us that clouds are the dust beneath the feet of God. On those days when we struggle to find relief from the heaviness and confusion of life, we need to remember that God is passing by. Sure, we may not be able to see or feel Him, but the clouds are the evidence of His presence, as are the whirlwind and the storm.

Let's take one more step in looking at the paths of God. Psalm 77:19 tells us, "Your way was in the sea And Your paths in the mighty waters, And Your footprints may not be known." The path that God chose for the Israelites to walk on led them to the Red Sea. Later, that path would lead them to the Jordan River. What are you to do when the path God walks on leads to unpassable obstacles? Water is not such an obstacle for the Lord. Emmanuel does not walk around water; He splits the seas and stops the rivers (Psalm 114:3). He walks on water (Matt. 14:25) and moves the mountains into the sea (Matt. 21:21). God is mightier than the breaker of the ocean (Psalm 93:3-4). The ways of God are not for the faint of heart, and that is why God desires to give His children new hearts and teach them to walk in His ways.

If we are to walk with Emmanuel, then we need to know Who He is and where His pathways are. But this is not the end. You can know who someone is, and you can know where they are; but as Amos 3:3 reminds us, that does not mean you have made an agreement with them.

The Agreement of Pace

Who a person is and the path they walk are only part of walking with someone. Truth be told, knowing these things about them are the most important to understanding that person; but if you are to walk with them, there is a great weight that falls on you. Pace is the speed in which the person is traveling. Pace is also the speed in which you must travel if you are to stay with them. What is God's pace? How fast is He going? How slow? Does God move in a literal sense or just figurative? These are great questions; but again, I'm going to let you walk through that with God. What I do see in Scripture is God does walk among us; and sometimes, He moves at different speeds.

Isaiah 40:31 says, "Yet those who wait for the LORD Will gain new strength; They will mount up with wings like eagles, They will run and not get tired, They will walk and not become weary." From this verse, we can see that God intends for us to go at different paces at different times. Let's break these down separately. First, we see that we are sometimes to wait on the Lord. These are those moments when God is giving us rest. There are many reasons why God has us wait. Maybe we are not ready to move forward. Possibly, the people there are not ready to be without us. Likewise, it could be that the people where we are headed are not ready for us to be there. It could be that God is working within His Church, so we wait. Or it could be that God is being patient with those in the world, not wanting to bring judgment before it is time. Waiting could be a building up or a storing up. It could be a tearing down or a slowing down. Not least among this list, waiting is often simply so that we can take time to get to know Emmanuel. "Cease *striving* and know that I am God; I will be exalted among the nations, I will be exalted in the earth" (Psalm 46:10).

Many are the reasons to wait; but often, we are not told which one applies to us. All we know is that God is not opening doors, nor is He moving, speaking, or giving. During seasons of waiting, it is easy to get impatient with God. We start to wander around trying to figure out the why. It is easy to wander into the pastures next to us because the grass looks greener. While we are supposed to be focusing on Emmanuel, we end up focusing on our own feelings and logic. Then we get discouraged and question God's goodness. In the end, we start questioning the reality of God, which leads to doubting, which leads to indifference, which leads to hate. When God has us wait, it is never so that we can do nothing. He always moves or doesn't move with a purpose. Waiting with Emmanuel is difficult, but it teaches us Who He is.

Another pace at which God moves is walking. All through Scripture, we are told to walk. Ephesians 5 tells us to walk three times. Walk in love (v. 2), walk as "children of light" (v. 8), and walk not as the unwise but as the wise (v. 15). Paul also told the church in Ephesus to walk in the manner in which you have been called (Eph. 4:1). Walking is the speed you go when you want to build a relationship. After Jesus rose from the dead, Jesus walked with two men for several miles while they discussed the events of the past several days (Luke 24:13-35). Jesus used that time to hear their hurts and even their budding doubts, and then He spoke healing words of truth. Walking with Emmanuel is life-giving.

Next, we see that God calls us to run. Again, we see throughout Scripture where God exhorts us to run. "Therefore, since we have so great a cloud of witnesses surrounding us, let us also lay aside every encumbrance and the sin which so easily entangles us, and let us run with endurance the race that is set before us" (Heb. 12:1). Running can be just as difficult as waiting. This is why the writer of Hebrews was saying to run the race with "endurance." Think about this, God has no need for energy because He does not grow weary or faint (Isa. 40:28).

So how is it that we are to keep up that pace with God? The answer to this lies not in our words but in God's presence. When we learn the discipline of enduring with Emmanuel, then we see that we do not grow weary or faint (Isa. 40:31). Therefore, we should run and run hard as long as God is running beside us. Do not seek the finite understanding of how this happens, but instead look at the heart of God and then press forward.

Paul says it this way: "Do you not know that those who run in a race all run, but *only* one receives the prize? Run in such a way that you may win. Everyone who competes in the games exercises self-control in all things. They then *do it* to receive a perishable wreath, but we an imperishable. Therefore I run in such a way, as not without aim; I box in such a way, as not beating the air" (I Cor. 9:24-26). Paul said to exercise self-control; this means that when your brain is telling you that you have nothing left, you have to trust God to either give you strength or give you rest. This is not a practice you can just will yourself to live out. Running with Emmanuel is something you will do every day of your life; and each time you determine to keep going in spite of the pain when you fall or think you can't go on, you are being lured into the wonder of God's glory. Running with Emmanuel teaches you His strength through your weakness.

Finally, the last pace God calls us to is rising up on wings like eagles. Another word for that is to "soar." When you are walking or running along with God and then He takes flight, hold on because He is doing something incredible. When God created us, He gave us limited abilities to wait, walk, and run; but He gave no provisions for us to fly. Yet we see in Scripture that sometimes He calls us up. "For by You I can run upon a troop; And by my God I can leap over a wall" (Psalm 18:29).

I do not know about you, but I cannot think of too many walls I can leap over. While I believe if God desires us to take flight, then we won't be able to stay on the ground, what He is probably saying here is the impossible will be done through those who wait on the Lord. However, I am not going to be the one who puts limits on Philippians 4:13: "I can do all things through Him who strengthens me." God's ways are not our ways (Isa. 55:8-9), and His paths are not the paths we normally walk. When God calls us to soar with Him, this means that He is breaking the mold on the very creation He created. This is no small thing. Be careful never to take ownership of these moments; falling from a standing position is very different from falling from the clouds. Soaring with Emmanuel is a lesson in trusting Him.

The Lure

What is the wonder God is luring us to when He offers for us to walk with Him? I believe the glorious wonder is in His very name, Emmanuel. When we understand God wants to be with us so much that He gave His Son in our place, that is when we begin to learn the character of God. That is when life begins to change. Try to imagine what life would be like if God was standing next to you. He could talk to you about the colors of the leaves, or He could show you the beauty of insects. Creation would come alive and dance before you for His glory.

The people around you would also be seen differently. Those who are thorns to you would begin to bloom with roses as Emmanuel tells you of His passion for them. Your choices would, in time, move from focusing on you and your wants to God and His glory. This is a discipline that must be learned, but what better way could we spend a lifetime? May we daily, even second by second, walk with Emmanuel.

Oh, Emmanuel,

*I do not believe I truly understand Your presence.
And as long as my flesh lives, I will never comprehend it.
So if I must die to self in order to walk with You,
then may I run to my cross, throw myself on it,
and wait for the resurrection. I never want to leave Your side.
Every moment of every day, I want to be aware of Your presence.
When you move, may I move. When you keep going,
may I endure. When you pull me back, may I not kick against You.
Please lure me into the wonder of walking with You.*

FOLLOWING THE LAMB

Roger looked over at his wife Noel, and they smiled at each other. They had been on an airplane for over twelve hours and still had a way to go, but it did not bother either one of them. They were so full of excitement and nerves that time was passing quickly. For a couple of years, they had been anticipating this very moment. After trying to have a child of their own and then going through the process of fertility tests, they had finally decided to pursue adoption. They had gone back and forth for weeks trying to decide whether to adopt domestically or internationally but had finally come to peace with adopting a child from Africa. They were headed to an orphanage, where they would meet the children and then decide who would be the newest member of their family. Roger and Noel held hands, overflowing with nervous energy and not able to sleep. Together, they waited.

"Children, come here," called Malindi. She was the house mother of the children at a small orphanage. She looked around at the young faces staring back at her as they sat on a dusty woven mat lying on the dirt floor. The kids had been running around while playing with a ball made out of discarded plastic bags, twine, and a shoe string. The kids were still breathing hard, and sweat rolled down their faces.

Malindi announced to the children that a family was coming later that day to see about adopting one of them. The children all began to whisper with excitement. Malindi instructed the kids to go clean their faces and to put on their school clothes. She also reminded them that it would be important to show respect to this couple by calling the man "sir" and the woman "ma'am." These strange English words did not roll off the children's tongues very easily, so they practiced saying them to each other.

Malindi laughed to herself as she listened to the chorus of mispronounced words. She hoped the couple would be good parents for her children. Though they were not her children, she had taken care of most of them ever since a war had destroyed a nearby village. Most of these kids knew each other and had been through enough pain. This couple was an opportunity to give a new life to one of these precious children.

When Roger and Noel arrived at the orphanage, they were brought into the room where the children usually ate their meals. An interpreter explained that Ms. Malindi had prepared the children to introduce themselves by saying a greeting, their name, and their age. Roger could already tell choosing was going to be an impossible task, and Noel was trying desperately to hold back her tears.

They watched with overwhelming anticipation as the first little boy stepped forward and said, *"Helu, sir and ma'am, mi nam is Mbutiabo. I am six."* Then he bashfully stepped back in line.

Next, a little girl stepped forward and said, *"Ma'am and shur, my name is Nandi. I am seven years."*

On down the line, the children stepped forward, told their information, and stepped back. Finally, the last little boy nervously stepped forward. His name was Matumbo, and he had practiced saying "sir" and "ma'am" with his friend, but he just could not get it right. Taking a deep breath, he looked at Roger and said, *"Sir."* Then looking at Noel, he said, *"Mom."*

The kids giggled at the slip-up, but Noel knew instantly that Matumbo was to be her little son. In that one word, she understood he could touch her very heart by knowing her name of love.

What's In a Name?

Jesus is known by many names in the Bible. Some of those names have verbal meanings like "Emmanuel" or "Alpha and Omega." But others have visual meanings such as "Root of Jesse" or "The Vine." Either way, Jesus is known and understood by His names. One of the names He is known by, which is not easily understood, comes from Revelation 5. This is an incredible account of John watching a mighty angel bring out a scroll that is sealed with seven seals. The angel cried out, asking who is worthy to open the scroll. But no one in Heaven was worthy. John began to weep until one of the elders told him to look at "The Lion of the Tribe of Judah." But when John looked, he did not see a lion but rather a "Lamb"—and not just any lamb, a mortally wounded lamb.

These two names for Jesus seem to give contrary information. The name "Lion of the Tribe of Judah" gives an understanding of respect, power, and authority; but the name "Lamb" gives the image of sacrifice, dependance, and humility—not to mention that a lamb with a mortal wound further emphasizes weakness. John was looking for someone stronger than the mighty angel who could open the sealed scroll; but when he was pointed to a lion, he only saw a wounded lamb. The wounded lamb made all the difference because that day, John learned the power of a heart of love.

The Lamb of God

Let's dive deeper into this name of Jesus. In John 1, we see where John the Baptist was standing with two of his disciples as Jesus passed by. John, seeing Him, said, "'Behold, the Lamb of God!'" The two disciples heard John say this, so they began to follow this Lamb of God. At this point, a beautifully Divine event took place: Jesus turned around to look at them. Why did Jesus turn around? Jesus knew they were there; He knew they were going to follow Him before they got out of bed that morning. Why didn't He just wait for them to catch up? I do not know, but I am so happy that Jesus sometimes changes the direction He is walking and turns around.

Jesus asked the two men what they wanted, and they asked Him where He was staying. His response was, "'Come and you will see.'" Can you imagine that invitation being extended to you? "Come take a walk with Me; and together, we will go to where I dwell." My heart beats faster just thinking about it. These two men followed Jesus, and they ended up at a house where they spent the rest of the day talking to Him and listening to His words. As soon as they left, the Bible says that one of the men, Andrew, ran to find his brother Simon because he believed he had found the Messiah Who was the Promised One from the beginning (Gen. 3:15). When we walk with the Lamb, we are changed. And that change overflows into the lives of those around us, and they are also changed.

A Lesson from the Lamb

One day after a storm, I was picking up some sticks in the yard. I was trying to use that time to talk to God. It was during this time that I heard God speak to me.

He asked, "Where am I?" This is a great question God likes to ask and a good one we can ask ourselves. Basically, the question is, "Where do you see the fingerprint of God?"

I looked around where I was picking up sticks and saw cars going by. I asked God, "Are You in the people going by?"

"No, that is My love."

I continued to look around. Seeing the sticks I was picking up, I asked, "Are You in this creation? The sticks and dirt? Even the life cycle of nature?"

"No," He said, "that is My provision."

I looked around again, but I could not come up with another answer. "I don't know. Where are You?" I asked.

"I'm in you."

That was a special moment because it was a reminder that the Holy Spirit of God dwells in all who know Him as their Savior. First Corinthians 6:19-20 says, "Or do you not know that your body is a temple of the Holy Spirit who is in you, whom you have from God, and that you are not your own? For you have been bought with a price: therefore glorify God in your body."

We are the physical temple of the Spirit of God. I took some time that day to meditate on this as I picked up sticks. Initially, as

I considered being the temple of God, I was excited; but as time went on, I began to think about all of the trials and pains I had gone through. I have scars that I carry with me. Some of these scars are self-induced from poor choices I have made; others are from walking through the briars of life. I do not make a very good temple for the God Who created me and saved me.

I asked God, "What about my scars?"

His response profoundly touched every one of those scars. He said, "I would not know you except through My scars. You would not know Me except through your scars. And life more abundant is the healing that comes from us walking together."

Just in case you missed that, let's break that down.

The Lamb's Scars

Isaiah 53:5 states, "But He was pierced through for our transgressions, He was crushed for our iniquities; The chastening for our well-being *fell* upon Him, And by His scourging we are healed." The wounds of Jesus ran much deeper than flesh and bone. In fact, if you want to know just how deep His wounds ran, we must become like doubting Thomas. At Thomas' request, the resurrected Jesus allowed him to put his finger in the nail holes and his hand where the spear had pierced Jesus' side (John 20:24-28).

John 19:34 says, "But one of the soldiers pierced His side with a spear, and immediately blood and water came out." Biology teaches that the water was present because of the body's response to the loss of blood and the stress that had been put on Jesus. Water would have collected around His heart and lungs so that when the soldier pierced Jesus' side, he also pierced that sack of water causing blood and water to come out. To understand the depth of Jesus' wounds, you must take them all the way to His heart. Once Thomas put his hand in the wound, it was as if he had touched the very heart of God because he cried out, "'My Lord and my God!'" When we touch the heart of God, we are then touched by His love.

Jesus showed me that day, while I picked up sticks, that He cannot know me because of my sin. God is holy and can no more be with sin any more than light can be with darkness. It was Jesus' scars that produced the cleansing blood that washed my sins away, making myself knowable to Him. The Lamb went to the cross so that we could be reconciled together.

My Scars

God knows me through His scars, and I can only know Him through my scars. How can someone know what healing is unless they have known hurt? How can they know resurrection unless they have known death? We cannot know peace unless we first know turmoil. Nor can we know forgiveness unless we first know condemnation. It is true that we have scars from our past, but it is through those scars that we can understand God's merciful touch. I believe this is why James can say, "Consider it all joy, my brethren, when you encounter various trials, knowing that the testing of your faith produces endurance. And let endurance have its perfect result, so that you may be perfect and complete, lacking in nothing" (James 1:2-4). James understood that the trials we go through produce scars, but those scars are the gateway though which God reveals His character.

What is the character of God? John 10:10 says, "The thief comes only to steal and kill and destroy; I came that they may have life, and have *it* abundantly." So, the character of the thief is death, hurt, and destruction; but the character of God is life, reconciliation, and healing. God disciplines us so that we do not walk away from Him, but He does not hurt us or tear us down. He is not about condemnation but instead restoration. Once we understand this, we can count our scars as joy because they draw us deeper to the heart of the Lamb.

HEALING TOGETHER

Finally, when God told me, "Life more abundant is the healing that comes from us walking together," I found a hope I had not known before. I know there is healing from our scars, but I always figured that came when we stepped into our new bodies. We catch a glimpse of our new bodies in II Corinthians 5:1-5:

> For we know that if the earthly tent which is our house is torn down, we have a building from God, a house not made with hands, eternal in the heavens. For indeed in this *house* we groan, longing to be clothed with our dwelling from heaven, inasmuch as we, having put it on, will not be found naked. For indeed while we are in this tent, we groan, being burdened, because we do not want to be unclothed but to be clothed, so that what is mortal will be swallowed up by life. Now He who prepared us for this very purpose is God, who gave to us the Spirit as a pledge.

Yet as I picked up sticks that day, God told me that healing does not have to wait for my new body; instead, healing could take place now. But it comes from walking with Him.

The Lion and The Lamb

When John was watching to see if there was anyone in Heaven who was worthy to open the scroll that was sealed, he heard about a Lion; but he saw a wounded Lamb (Rev. 5:1-10). Often in life, we find ourselves surrounded by hurts, scars, pain, and uncertainty. We cry out to God to save us, to be our Refuge, and to be our Strong Tower. We look to Scripture, and we see instances when God helped a little boy kill a giant (1 Sam. 17). We see when He walked with three men in a fiery furnace (Dan. 3). We can see a dead Lazarus walking out of a grave (John 11). In our heart of hearts, we truly believe God is still the Lion of the Tribe of Judah. He can still do what we cannot. His power, His wisdom, and His authority are still enough to save us from our life of death. But when God reveals Himself in our lives, He appears to be a wounded Lamb.

What is it about our Savior being a Lion that brings you comfort in times of trial? What is it about Him being a slain Lamb that causes doubt to creep in? What happens to your spirit when you realize that the slain Lamb is standing, risen from the dead, and now victorious over death?

_____

_____

_____

_____

The Lure

God longs for us to know Him as The Lion, but we cannot know His power until we can trust His worthiness to open the scroll. You cannot see the Lion until you can go through the wounds of the Lamb. To say it another way, you cannot know God's name of authority until you can speak His name of Love. The Lamb knows you intimately only because of His saving wounds. Likewise, we can only know Him through our wounded, helpless, and broken lives. This is not a one-time, five-minute, get-to-know-you event. No, this is a discipline of learning to follow the Lamb.

When Andrew heard John the Baptist say, "The Lamb of God," he was so lured into the wonder of God that he followed Jesus into His dwelling presence. When God does not seem to be enough to save you from the hurt and trials of life, do not lose heart; press deeper into the wounds of the Lamb because that is where you will find the heart of the Lion. Literally, when life seems to be too much, fall on your face before Jesus and begin praising Him for His sacrifice on the cross. Do not stop praising Him until the Lamb roars as a Lion!

What does this mean? Try to imagine a life surrounded by trials, but instead of cowering to the threat, you praise the Lamb Who is greater than the weight of this world. The wounded Lamb is greater than cancer, stronger than anxieties, and holds more authority than mourning. I am not saying that you will no longer feel pain or hurt. Following the Lamb does not stop tribulation. Following the Lamb leads us into trials, but it is there that we learn His character, which teaches us that His name brings healing. "Because he has loved Me, therefore I will deliver him; I will set him *securely* on high, because he has known My name. He will call upon Me, and I will answer him; I will be with him in trouble; I will rescue him and honor him" (Psalm 91:14-15).

O Lamb of God,
Most of the time I am looking for a Lion
Who will take away the pain I feel.
But so often, You reveal Yourself to me as a Lamb.
I'm so sorry I do not trust the wounded
Lamb to have the strength to take care of my issues.
May I look past my circumstances,
through Your wounds, and straight to Your heart,
which beats ferociously with love for me.

ABIDING ON THE VINE

Many years ago, a monk sat quietly in his small room while he copied Scripture. The only furnishings in his room were a bed and a simple desk. He sat at the desk where a candle flickered. The air was crisp that evening as the monk looked up from his copying and looked out his window at the fresh blanket of snow in the courtyard. His life was a simple one; but he was warm and well-fed, and his days were filled with opportunities to grow closer to God.

All of a sudden, the door to his room burst open; and a filthy man wearing all black rushed in and slammed back the door. In the amount of time it took the monk's candle to flicker, the dirty man had rushed across the room and held a dagger to the monk's throat. "You will hide me here, or I will kill you!"

The monk, though startled at the disturbance, was at peace as he told the man, "You are welcome to stay here as long as you desire; and you have my word that I will make no attempts to alert anyone, nor will I inquire as to why you are on the run on such a cold evening. Please follow me, and I will get you some food and a place to sleep."

The stranger did not trust the monk, but he did not have a lot of options.

"My name is Andrew," said the monk as they entered the small kitchen, where a wood burning stove was already hot.

"My name is none of your concern," growled the man.

"Very well, then. I will call you Jacob." Andrew smiled as he handed the man a hot bowl of soup. "I think it is important for me to tell you that this snow falling tonight will block you within my walls until spring comes and melts it. But I assure you that I have plenty of food and wood to keep you fed and warm through the winter. If you stay through the night, you will have to stay through the winter. If you choose to leave, you will probably be captured or frozen to death by morning."

Jacob thought for a moment, weighing his options, but decided lying low for a few months might not be that bad.

Unknown to Jacob, Andrew's house had only one bed; and his pantry only had enough food for the monk. Andrew gave Jacob his bed and bid him good night. That night, Andrew prayed into the wee hours of the morning for God to work in Jacob's heart, no matter what it might cost him. Making a small pallet in the kitchen, Andrew lay down and fell asleep.

The morning came early along with deep snow. Andrew gathered his bedding long before his guest woke up. By the time Jacob stumbled out of his room, Andrew had breakfast ready and hot. Andrew served his guest and provided for his needs before he continued to carry on his daily chores of splitting the wood, cleaning the house, preparing the meals, shoveling snow, and copying Scripture. This was the pattern that followed day in and day out for a couple months; Andrew worked, served, and prayed, while Jacob watched and napped.

One night while Jacob slept in his bed, he was startled awake by a crashing sound. He got out of bed and searched through the house for Andrew. He found him convulsing on his pallet in front of the kitchen stove. Jacob rushed over to him and found that he was burning with fever. He did not really know what to do, so he grabbed a wet rag and placed it on the trembling monk's face.

Andrew weakly grabbed Jacob's hand and held on. The whole time he had been there, Jacob had not once noticed how bone-thin Andrew's hands and arms were. In fact, Andrew was not much more than a skeleton. Jacob asked Andrew what he should do, but the monk's words were too weak to be heard. Then his eyes rolled back, and he became unconscious.

Jacob tried to think about what Andrew would do if it were he who was unconscious, but he didn't know. He decided to get Andrew in bed. Why had he been lying on the floor, anyway? Jacob realized that he had never even bothered to look around the house. He ran around searching every closed door for Andrew's bedroom, only to find that the only bed in the house was his own. Jacob was astonished that Andrew would willingly and silently give up his own bed so a criminal could have a place to sleep. He quickly carried Andrew to the bed and gently laid him down and covered him up.

The next day, Jacob went to the kitchen to find some breakfast. He looked in the pantry, only to find most of the shelves were bare. Instantly, he understood that Andrew had said he had enough food for both of them but only because he had been going without. That would explain his boney hands.

The next day, Jacob tended to Andrew, cleaning him and making sure he seemed comfortable. That evening, he tiredly lay on the pallet in the kitchen floor and watched the shadows dance on the walls as the candle flickered until he fell asleep.

Days passed before Andrew woke up. Weeks passed; and Jacob busied himself splitting wood, fixing meals, and tidying up the house. He couldn't decide if his mind was becoming blurrier or clearer. Often, he did not know if he was talking to himself or talking to God as he had seen Andrew do so often.

One day, as Jacob was baking some bread, he was startled to hear a knock at the outside gate. Even though Andrew was getting better, he was in no shape to walk through the cool courtyard. Jacob knew that someone knocking must mean that spring had melted the snow and he would be free to go. He slowly opened the heavy, wooden door and found himself standing face to face with the police chief. Jacob's heart sank. He was totally exposed.

"Good morning, Father Andrew, my old friend," the police chief said with a hearty laugh. "It is good to see that you have weathered the winter snows with no ill effect. And it smells as if you are baking that delicious bread of yours."

Jacob did not know what to say. He simply nodded.

The police chief continued, "Well, I just wanted to check on you. I look forward to eating some of your garden vegetables when harvest comes around. Goodbye."

Jacob thanked the police chief and closed the door.

Standing in the doorway of the kitchen was Andrew, smiling. "My son, you have learned to serve. You have learned to love. You are no longer recognized as the dirty man who burst into my home all those nights ago."

Jacob understood; he had spent so much time with Andrew that he now looked and served just like him.

Walking in the Spirit

Oftentimes, it is the silent work of God that speaks the loudest. We can see people's actions, and we can hear their words; but we are not able to see or hear what God is doing in their spirit. "God is spirit" (John 4:24), and that is why God does not usually connect to us in our physical senses. Instead, he connects with us in our spiritual senses. We must learn to "walk by the Spirit" (Gal. 5:16). This is a huge struggle for many Christians. How do we live in a physical world but operate in our spirit? When we desire for God to move in our lives, we long to see the physical changes; but we overlook the spiritual stirring. Change will often start with a stirring of our spirit as God interacts and reveals Himself to us. Once our spirit is engaged, then it will move to our physical body.

Usually, we want change to be immediate, not jarring nor requiring a lot of work or sacrifice. We simply want to be changed from the comfort of our recliner. We do not want others to see that we need to be changed, so we do not want God to rock the boat. We do not want to go to classes about our addictions. We do not want to give up the technology that brings porn into our homes. Change is something we just want God to produce in us. But that is not usually how the Vinedresser tends His vineyard.

The Vine

Let's dive deeper into this understanding of a life-changing journey with the Spirit. John 15:1-11 speaks of our relationship to God as one of a vine in a vineyard. The Father is the Vinedresser; Jesus is the Vine; the Spirit of God is the Grower of the fruit; and we are a branch on the Vine. There is a whole life-giving relationship that transpires as the Vinedresser interacts with the branches so that the Spirit can produce a likeness to the Vine in us. John 15:5 says, "I am the vine, you are the branches; he who abides in Me and I in him, he bears much fruit, for apart from Me you can do nothing." Our spirit is the point where the branch and the vine connect. The Vinedresser interacts with our finite lives by washing and pruning, while the Spirit works in our spirit, so that we can grow in our Christlikeness. This process should be as natural as an apple tree producing apples. They do not appear overnight but are instead grown through a season of connectedness.

What does Jesus mean when He says, "He who abides in Me and I in him?" What does it mean to abide? Let's start by looking at what it is not. Abiding is not your daily quiet time. I do not care if your daily quiet time lasts for three hours or three minutes. It is not going to church. It does not matter if you are at church every time the doors are open. None of these mean you are abiding with God.

The best way I can describe this to you is through the many families who will go and cut down their Christmas tree during the Christmas season. They will bring it home and put it in water so that it will stay green and fresh. If I were to ask you if they had a living Christmas tree, you might say "yes" because it is not artificial. But that tree is far from "living." In fact, that tree ceased to be alive the very moment the trunk was cut from its life source. Likewise, we may interact with God through our quiet time or worship at church; but the moment we get up and break our connection to God, we have severed ourselves from our Life source.

What is the answer then? Are we to have a twenty-four hour-a-day quiet time or live at church? No, our spirit is to remain connected to the Spirit of God at all times. Everywhere we go and in everything we do, our spirit is to abide with the Vine. This is a discipline that could take years to gain ground in because we are so easily distracted. How do we stay connected to God at a football game or while on a date? It is easier to segment life in the categories of spiritual life and daily life. Truly, the world around us does not mind a little religion, as long as it does not cross a line. Abiding on the Vine will require that we live differently than the world.

The Spirit's Fruit

Imagine finding a magic lamp with a genie inside who said, "I'll give you five wishes." What would you ask for? Use the lines below to list out your top five wishes:

_____

_____

_____

_____

_____

After you have made your list, take a moment and try to figure out what the common threads are within your list. These common threads will probably reveal what it is you really want. For example, you may have said you want a new boat; but what you are really wanting is to get away from your stressful job and do something you enjoy. You may have listed healing from a sickness, but what you really want is to joyfully live an unhindered life. You may have said you wanted more wishes, but what you are really saying is that there are things in your life you would really like changed if you could. This might take some time to work through, but I believe what we say we want is really just a stepping stone to what our heart really desires.

Our wishes may surface as physical objects or emotional relief; but really, at their root, our desires are spiritual. Physical and emotional fulfillment is temporary. Our likes and dislikes change as we grow, and our mood changes with the rise and fall of our feelings. But our spirits are eternal; they long for things which will not pass away. What then is it that we really want? In Scripture, there is a list of eternal gifts which are not so much given as they are grown on the Vine: "love, joy, peace, patience, kindness, goodness, faithfulness, gentleness, self-control" (Gal. 5:22-23). These are the fruits of the Spirit. These are what the Spirit grows in us when we abide on the Vine. Is it not true that what we spend our money on are the things we hope will make our lives easier, so we can have a moment's peace? Or we arrange our calendar, so we can fit in the activities we like and experience some joy among the chaos. We search for someone who will be faithful, kind, and gentle to us because that is love. God knows we are filled with so much want, but the fruit of His presence is what is at the root of our desire.

Pollinating the Fruit

There are varieties of fruit trees that cannot bear fruit unless they have been cross-pollinated. For example, most apple trees cannot bear apples unless another apple tree of a different variety is growing near them. This is so bees can take pollen from one to the other. The bee cannot take pollen from a peach tree and put it on the blossom of an apple tree and have an apple grow. That's not how God designed these trees to work. One apple tree's pollen grows another apple tree's apples.

Spiritually, we cannot grow the fruit of peace unless we have been pollinated by another tree's peace. The peace of the world is not really peace because only Jesus gives real peace (John 14:27). Truly, if we are to grow the fruit of the Spirit, then we must abide in the fruit of the Vine. What does this mean? We will not grow love unless we spend time in the love of God. We will not grow kindness unless we abide in the kindness of God. We cannot display faithfulness unless we live day to day in the faithfulness of God. Abiding in God is how we are cross-pollinated by His fruit.

The following verses are not meant to speak about you; but rather, they speak of the character of God. Jesus said, "'If you abide in Me, and My words abide in you, ask whatever you wish, and it will be done for you'" (John 15:7). These verses drip with the pollen of the fruit of the Spirit. Take time to meditate on God's words, memorize them, abide in them, and declare them daily.

Love
- **John 3:16:** "For God so loved the world, that He gave His only begotten Son, that whoever believes in Him shall not perish, but have eternal life."
- **I John 4:16:** "We have come to know and have believed the love which God has for us. God is love, and the one who abides in love abides in God, and God abides in him."

- **Romans 5:8:** "But God demonstrates His own love toward us, in that while we were yet sinners, Christ died for us."
- **Galatians 2:20:** "I have been crucified with Christ; and it is no longer I who live, but Christ lives in me; and the *life* which I now live in the flesh I live by faith in the Son of God, who loved me and gave Himself up for me."
- **I John 3:1:** "See how great a love the Father has bestowed on us, that we would be called children of God; and *such* we are. For this reason the world does not know us, because it did not know Him."

Joy

- **Hebrews 12:2:** "Fixing our eyes on Jesus, the author and perfecter of faith, who for the joy set before Him endured the cross, despising the shame, and has sat down at the right hand of the throne of God."
- **Nehemiah 8:10:** "Then he said to them, 'Go, eat of the fat, drink of the sweet, and send portions to him who has nothing prepared; for this day is holy to our Lord. Do not be grieved, for the joy of the LORD is your strength.'"
- **Psalm 16:11:** "You will make known to me the path of life; In Your presence is fullness of joy; In Your right hand there are pleasures forever."
- **Philippians 4:4:** "Rejoice in the Lord always; again I will say, rejoice!"
- **John 15:11:** "These things I have spoken to you so that My joy may be in you, and *that* your joy may be made full."
- **Zephaniah 3:17:** "The LORD your God is in your midst, A victorious warrior. He will exult over you with joy, He

will be quiet in His love, He will rejoice over you with shouts of joy."

Peace

- **Philippians 4:6-7:** "Be anxious for nothing, but in everything by prayer and supplication with thanksgiving let your requests be made known to God. And the peace of God, which surpasses all comprehension, will guard your hearts and your minds in Christ Jesus."
- **II Thessalonians 3:16:** "Now may the Lord of peace Himself continually grant you peace in every circumstance. The Lord be with you all!"
- **Colossians 3:15:** "Let the peace of Christ rule in your hearts, to which indeed you were called in one body; and be thankful."
- **Isaiah 26:3:** "The steadfast of mind You will keep in perfect peace, Because he trusts in You."
- **John 14:27:** "Peace I leave with you; My peace I give to you; not as the world gives do I give to you. Do not let your heart be troubled, nor let it be fearful."
- **I Thessalonians 5:23:** "Now may the God of peace Himself sanctify you entirely; and may your spirit and soul and body be preserved complete, without blame at the coming of our Lord Jesus Christ."

Patience

- **II Peter 3:9:** "The Lord is not slow about His promise, as some count slowness, but is patient toward you, not wishing for any to perish but for all to come to repentance."

- **I Timothy 1:16:** "Yet for this reason I found mercy, so that in me as the foremost, Jesus Christ might demonstrate His perfect patience as an example for those who would believe in Him for eternal life."
- **Joel 2:13:** "'And rend your heart and not your garments.' Now return to the LORD your God, For He is gracious and compassionate, Slow to anger, abounding in lovingkindness And relenting of evil."
- **Isaiah 40:31:** "Yet those who wait for the LORD Will gain new strength; They will mount up with wings like eagles, They will run and not get tired, They will walk and not become weary."
- **James 5:7-8:** "Therefore be patient, brethren, until the coming of the Lord. The farmer waits for the precious produce of the soil, being patient about it, until it gets the early and late rains. You too be patient; strengthen your hearts, for the coming of the Lord is near."
- **II Peter 3:15:** "And regard the patience of our Lord as salvation; just as also our beloved brother Paul, according to the wisdom given him, wrote to you."

Kindness

- **Psalm 63:3:** "Because Your lovingkindness is better than life, My lips will praise You."
- **Titus 3:4-6:** "But when the kindness of God our Savior and *His* love for mankind appeared, He saved us, not on the basis of deeds which we have done in righteousness, but according to His mercy, by the washing of regeneration and

renewing by the Holy Spirit, whom He poured out upon us richly through Jesus Christ our Savior."
- **Psalm 36:7:** "How precious is Your lovingkindness, O God! And the children of men take refuge in the shadow of Your wings."
- **Romans 2:4:** "Or do you think lightly of the riches of His kindness and tolerance and patience, not knowing that the kindness of God leads you to repentance?"

Goodness
- **I Chronicles 16:34:** "O give thanks to the LORD, for *He is* good; For His lovingkindness is everlasting."
- **Psalm 25:8:** "Good and upright is the LORD; Therefore He instructs sinners in the way."
- **Psalm 143:10:** "Teach me to do Your will, For You are my God; Let Your good Spirit lead me on level ground."
- **Mark 10:18:** "And Jesus said to him, "Why do you call Me good? No one is good except God alone."
- **Psalm 27:13:** *"I would have despaired* unless I had believed that I would see the goodness of the LORD In the land of the living."
- **Psalm 145:5-7:** "On the glorious splendor of Your majesty And on Your wonderful works, I will meditate. Men shall speak of the power of Your awesome acts, And I will tell of Your greatness. They shall eagerly utter the memory of Your abundant goodness And will shout joyfully of Your righteousness."
- **Nahum 1:7:** "The LORD is good, A stronghold in the day of trouble, And He knows those who take refuge in Him."

Faithfulness

- **I Corinthians 10:13:** "No temptation has overtaken you but such as is common to man; and God is faithful, who will not allow you to be tempted beyond what you are able, but with the temptation will provide the way of escape also, so that you will be able to endure it."
- **I John 1:9:** "If we confess our sins, He is faithful and righteous to forgive us our sins and to cleanse us from all unrighteousness."
- **I Corinthians 1:9:** "God is faithful, through whom you were called into fellowship with His Son, Jesus Christ our Lord."
- **II Timothy 2:13:** "If we are faithless, He remains faithful, for He cannot deny Himself."
- **II Thessalonians 3:3:** "But the Lord is faithful, and He will strengthen and protect you from the evil *one*."
- **I Thessalonians 5:23-24:** "Now may the God of peace Himself sanctify you entirely; and may your spirit and soul and body be preserved complete, without blame at the coming of our Lord Jesus Christ. Faithful is He who calls you, and He also will bring it to pass."
- **Lamentations 2:22-23:** "The LORD's lovingkindnesses indeed never cease, For His compassions never fail. *They* are new every morning; Great is Your faithfulness."

Gentleness

- **Isaiah 30:18:** "Therefore the LORD longs to be gracious to you, And therefore He waits on high to have compassion on you. For the LORD is a God of justice; How blessed are all those who long for Him."

- **I Kings 19:12:** "After the earthquake a fire, *but* the LORD *was* not in the fire; and after the fire a sound of a gentle blowing."
- **Matthew 11:29:** "Take My yoke upon you and learn from Me, for I am gentle and humble in heart, and YOU WILL FIND REST FOR YOUR SOULS."
- **Matthew 21:4-5:** "This took place to fulfill what was spoken through the prophet: "SAY TO THE DAUGHTER OF ZION, 'BEHOLD YOUR KING IS COMING TO YOU, GENTLE, AND MOUNTED ON A DONKEY, EVEN ON A COLT, THE FOAL OF A BEAST OF BURDEN.'"

Self-Control
- **II Timothy 1:7:** "For God has not given us a spirit of timidity, but of power and love and discipline."
- **James 1:19-20:** "*This* you know, my beloved brethren. But everyone must be quick to hear, slow to speak *and* slow to anger; for the anger of man does not achieve the righteousness of God."
- **I Peter 5:6:** "Therefore humble yourselves under the mighty hand of God, that He may exalt you at the proper time."

My prayer is that you would be cross-pollinated by the fruit of the Spirit, so you can bear fruit in line with the God-given desires of your heart (Psalm 37:4). This is a discipline that we must daily practice. When I abide in the self-control of God, then I will also act in self-control. This principle is paramount; I cannot live a life of peace, joy, love, or kindness unless I am close enough to the Vine to get cross-pollinated by Jesus' fruit.

The Lure

Most human beings will spend every day of their life looking for purpose and trying to buy their desires; but at the root of it, what we desire is only found in God. Life, love, and hope are all laced into the very being of Jesus Christ. As we abide with the Vine, we spend time in the kindness and joy of His presence, which then produces kindness and joy in us through the work of the Spirit. While we are growing these fruits, the Vinedresser is washing and pruning us so that we will grow even more fruit. What could be better?

As we spend time in the peace of God, He grows our peace. As we grow in the peace of God, He produces more peace in us. Our search for peace does not end in a self-help book or the latest gadget, and it does not cost us a penny or require that we subscribe to someone's products. Peace, along with love and joy, are grown in us when we learn the discipline of abiding in the presence of God. As you abide on the Vine, you will begin to see more of the fruit of the Vine produced in your life.

Oh, Vinedresser,
May we not listen to the lies of the devil.
We cannot find peace anywhere other than your presence.
Love from any other source is a fabrication and doomed
to leave us lacking. True authentic fruit is not found;
it is grown over time as we are pollinated by the fruit of Your Spirit.
May we abide on Your Vine.

ALIGNING WITH THE CORNERSTONE

    Chester Smith was a young man who most would say was "blessed." He was married and had two beautiful daughters. They lived in a cozy house in a nice neighborhood. His daughters liked to play on the swing set he had made for them where his wife could watch them from the kitchen window. Chester had a good job working at a warehouse. The pay wasn't much, but it provided for his family. All in all, Chester was blessed.

    But Chester also had a little secret, a vise you might call it. When he was in college, some friends had invited him to hangout. When he got there, his best friend had pulled out a case of beer; and everyone had begun passing them around. Chester had never drunk alcohol before; not because he was against it, but he just never wanted to. But he hadn't wanted the other guys to tease him, so he had taken the can and begun to drink it.

    Something inside him had changed that day. He was never really able to explain it, but everything about that can of beer brought out something wonderful inside him. As time went by, he found that the euphoria he felt after one beer was doubled after the second one.

This began a pattern of drinking, which landed him as a functional alcoholic. He would go to work each day and work hard, and then he would come home and be "dad." But after the girls went to bed, Chester would begin to drink until late in the night. This was Chester's routine; and though he no longer felt the euphoria, he just couldn't stop drinking.

Finally, one day during a stressful time at work, Chester found himself drinking while on his lunch break. When he got back to work, he couldn't think straight; his mind just struggled to keep up; and his words hung in his mouth like molasses. While driving the forklift, Chester turned a little too slowly and ended up knocking over several pallets of chemicals, nearly running into a co-worker. Chester's boss came over and could smell the alcohol on his breath. He was fired immediately.

Chester struggled to go home that afternoon. He just couldn't bring himself to tell his wife what had happened. He spent the afternoon down at a bar, crawling deeper into a bottle. Finally, after 8:00, Chester stumbled through the front door, where his very worried family rushed to him. His wife already knew what had happened at work because she had called his boss when he hadn't come home. She tried to console him, but he was too embarrassed to talk about it. He couldn't even look at his little girls.

The next day, he vowed to make it right, but no job was to be found. Days turned into weeks, which became months; and still, he felt the shame of being jobless. He began drinking again to cope with the shame but nothing like the day when the call came that the bank was foreclosing on their house. Chester's family went to live with his in-laws, but he just got in his car and drove to the liquor store. That night, in a drunken stupor, he passed out on the sidewalk and, for the first time, experienced homelessness.

Chester never went back to his family; he trolled the streets during the day looking for something to drink and then passed out somewhere each night. Sometimes, he slept in a vacant lot and sometimes on a park bench, but he was lost deep in the regret of his life. He had found that living in a big city provided more places to sleep and more opportunities to drink. It also helped that no one knew who he once was.

One night, he staggered down a street nicknamed "The Morgue," so called because so many homicides happened on this street that the morgue wouldn't even come to get the bodies until morning. It was just too dangerous. Chester staggered down the street as a car squealed its tires turning onto the far end of the street. The car raced down the street nearly out of control and, at the last second, swerved and hit Chester. He smashed into the hood and flew over the windshield, landing on the road, bleeding and broken. The car never even slowed down.

That same night, a small intercity church was holding a revival service. The speaker was a country pastor, who lived a couple hours away. He had left the church and was eagerly trying to get home. He had made a wrong turn and was trying to find the best way back on track when he found himself driving down "The Morgue." Up ahead, the pastor could see something in the road; and as he drove nearer, he could see that it was a man. The pastor didn't know where he was, but he knew enough to understand that if he stopped, he very well could end up just like this poor man. The pastor did the only thing he knew to do: he prayed for the broken man. He didn't know if the man was alive or dead, but he pulled over to the other side of the road and drove past.

Shortly after that pastor had left the small intercity church, an elder locked up and began to head home. The elder mindlessly drove down "The Morgue" just like he had done hundreds of times on his way home. But this night, he could see something in the road. As he drew near, he could tell it was Chester. The elder didn't really know Chester, but he had seen him standing on street corners. The elder's heart broke seeing his tattered jacket and ripped jeans. He knew it was far too dangerous to stop, so he did what he knew to do: he prayed for the broken homeless man in the road. He pulled over to the other side of the road and continued home.

That same night, a Muslim named Mahammad Akbar was in the city on business. He had finished eating his dinner at a restaurant and was now driving back to his hotel. He watched the GPS screen as it told him to turn left. He drove down "The Morgue" and quickly surmised that this was not a safe place. Up ahead, he could see something in the road, but he was not interested in the scenery. He just wanted to get out of the area and on to the safety of his hotel where he was supposed to call his wife when he got in. As he neared the crumpled mess in the road, Mahammad could see that it was a man. His heart broke for him. Quickly, he looked around to see if anyone else might be coming to help this man, but no one was around. He looked around again to see if anyone might be watching to attack him if he stopped. Again, no one was nearby.

Finally, against his better judgment, Mahammad stopped his car in the middle of the street and got out to check on Chester. There was a lot of blood coming from a wound with exposed bone. Chester was unconscious and barely breathing. Quickly, he pulled out his cell phone and called 911. He told the operator what little he knew of his location and the condition of the man. She assured him that help would come; but because of a major accident on the interstate, all of the ambulances were in use. He would need to stay with Chester and apply pressure to his wounds.

Mahammad looked around again before running to the back of his car to get his sports coat. He laid it on Chester to keep him warm, and then he began to rip the bottom of his shirt to have something to press against the wound. While he waited, Mahammad began to talk to Chester. He talked about his family, his job, his religion, and anything else to take his mind off what was going on.

Finally, four hours later, an ambulance pulled up; and a couple EMTs jumped out to help. They moved Chester onto a stretcher and put him in the ambulance, and then they rushed to the hospital. Mahammad didn't know what to do, so he followed the ambulance. He sat up all night waiting to hear what was going on. At last, a doctor came to him and explained that Chester had survived but was in critical condition.

Mahammad's business trip still had several days; and each day when he got off, he would go to the hospital to check on Chester. Even after his trip ended, he would call the hospital for updates. Chester regained consciousness and even began to get better. Finally, the day came for him to be released from the hospital. He could not walk and had no money to get the therapy he needed to regain that ability.

When Mahammad heard that Chester was being released without further help, he and his wife both got in the car and drove to the city and picked him up. He would go and live with Mahammad's family, and they would provide for his therapy.

Many months later, Chester was able to walk with a cane and care for his basic needs. A small apartment had become available near Mahammad's family, and Chester wanted to start a new life. He had now been sober for several months and felt that maybe this time, he could move past his vise. Mahammad and Chester remained as close as brothers. They shared life together; and through the years, they walked through pain and joy, hurt and healing.

Now, I ask you, of the pastor, the elder, or the Muslim, who loved Chester? "'Go and do the same'" (Luke 10:37).

In Line with the Cornerstone

Several years ago, I had the privilege of going to Juarez, Mexico, with a small organization to build houses. We had groups of teenagers come to us, and we would teach them to lay a very simple cinderblock house. Even though I am not a block layer, nor do I know anything about construction, I was put in charge of the worksite. I would teach the groups about mixing the mortar and troweling it on the blocks, as well as how to use a tightly pulled string to lay the blocks so they were level. The technique was to make sure the edge of your block touched the string. If you were above or below the string, you needed to keep leveling.

One day, during a break, some of the missionaries who had been working on these houses all summer decided we would catch up the group by laying the blocks ourselves without the string. We would quickly trowel the mortar, lay the block, check it with a level, and then move on. We discovered after several rows of cinderblocks had been laid that we had laid level blocks, but they were not in line with the corner stone. Our wall had a curve in it which would cause it to collapse if it was not fixed. This was a humiliating moment for us as we had to explain to our boss, the group of teenagers, and the angry owner of the house the mistake we had made. Aligning with the cornerstone means the difference between a house which stands and a house which crumbles.

The Corner of What?

Jesus was teaching in the temple one day when the chief priest and the elders came to Him asking by what authority He was doing His works. Jesus' response, as usual, was to tell a parable. He told of a man who owned a vineyard. The man prepared the land, dug a winepress, and built a tower. The man then rented the vineyard out to some farmers before he went away on a trip. The farmers tended the vines and reaped a harvest. When the owner sent slaves to collect his portion of the harvest, the farmers beat a slave, stoned a slave, and killed another. The landowner sent another group of slaves, and the same thing happened. Finally, the owner sent his son, demanding respect, but the farmers threw out the son and killed him, too.

Then Jesus asked the religious leaders what they thought the landowner would do to these farmers? They responded with the ideas of contempt, condemnation, and revenge. Jesus then revealed His purpose by quoting from Psalm 118:22-23, "The stone which the builders rejected Has become the chief corner *stone*. This is the LORD'S doing; It is marvelous in our eyes." The religious leaders understood from this verse that Jesus was referring to them as the farmers. This fueled their disdain for Him, and they looked for a way to get Him (Matt. 21:33-46).

But what did the verses from Psalm 118 mean? Why did it produce such hatred? To understand this, we need to understand the pieces of the puzzle. In these two verses, there are builders, stones, and a cornerstone. Let's break down this analogy.

The builders are building a structure, and they are using stones as the building blocks. They are looking for certain stones, ones that fit in line with the stone next to it. The structure they are building needs to be straight and strong; for this reason, only the "best" stones were chosen. Eventually, they came upon a stone that really did not fit the mold. Instead of being a stone that would keep the wall straight, it was a stone that turned. Therefore, they discarded that stone as useless. Eventually, another builder came along and took up this discarded stone and saw that it was exactly what was needed to be the cornerstone for their structure. Their structure would not be a straight wall but rather a spiritual house (I Peter 2:4-9). Walls are designed to separate those outside from those within, but this temple would be designed so everyone could come and worship God.

But for those who would reject God, they would trip over this cornerstone and be broken (Isa. 8:15). The builders of the wall were the religious leaders; the stones they were using were Jews; and the standard they used to choose stones was the Law. This is why they rejected the one stone. Jesus was a Jew who did not fit their mold. But God had placed Jesus in Zion to be the very Cornerstone of His Church. But to have a corner, there must be two walls coming together. The two walls are the Jews and the Gentiles (Eph. 2:19-22).

Through God's great plan, He had chosen a family and made them into a nation. That nation would then reject Him, and God would use the people He had not chosen to bring His beloved back to Him. You and I are the living stones which the Builder is using to build up this spiritual house. He aligns us with the Cornerstone and builds us upon His foundation. God is fitting Jews and Gentiles together as two walls coming together in a corner which is built on the cornerstone.

Jesus just did not fit what the spiritual leaders were expecting, and it just didn't make sense to them. What are some things about Jesus that just do not make sense for you?

_____

_____

_____

_____

_____

Building the Temple

God, in His holiness, cannot be in the same place as evil. For this reason, He is a Builder Who builds a wall of separation, evil on one side and righteousness on the other. But He did not stop with just a wall. He put in a corner so that the wall could be a building—a house, rather—which is available for all those who come through His gate. This house of worship would be for all people, Jew and Gentile alike. This blueprint did not sit well with the religious leaders, but it was the very structure they could not topple over. Their rejection of Jesus was the mortar which set Him in place as the Cornerstone. God builds this house of worship, but the question for you is whether you are being lured into the wonder of His presence. Have you lifted up your soul in worship to the Cornerstone?

Joining Two Walls of Worship

Jesus looked across a well at a sinful woman from Samaria and spoke of true worship. This worship was not divided into categories of Jew and Gentile, men and women, slave and free, or East and West. Jesus told her, "'But an hour is coming, and now is, when the true worshipers will worship the Father in spirit and truth; for such people the Father seeks to be His worshipers. God is spirit, and those who worship Him must worship in spirit and truth'" (John 4:23-24). Those who are to worship God in the spiritual house whose Cornerstone is Jesus Christ are to worship Him "in spirit and in truth." Again, Jesus is the joining of two walls, which houses the worship of the Father.

Spirit and Truth

For some time, I keep finding myself caught between two seemingly opposing religious forces. These two entities both worship Jesus as the only way to salvation; both meet in church buildings, sing songs, pray, and read the Bible. Both serve those in need, and both desire to worship God above all else. But it is rare for these two groups to worship together for very long.

I grew up and have served in Southern Baptist churches for my entire life. As a Southern Baptist, I have become well acquainted with learning the books of the Bible, doing sword drills, memorizing Scripture, and going to Bible studies. We are known as "The People of the Book" because that is what has been stressed from little children up to senior adults. But when I was in college, I found myself at a worship time rather different from what I was used to. As I sat there, the worship leader began to speak gibberish, which I have since learned was speaking in tongues, while the girl sitting next to me slid down on the floor laughing uncontrollably. People began to run up and down the aisles, dancing and lifting their hands while they sang. People began to prophesy and speak of things no one understood. Needless to say, I was uncomfortable and confused.

I went home and began talking to people I trusted, but the conversation became almost combative as I tried to find understanding. Since then, I have talked to pastors who have become angry as I asked questions pertaining to the moving of the Spirit and the use of certain spiritual gifts. Why? Jesus and the apostles healed the sick and raised the dead. Many people in the Old Testament prophesied and saw miracles take place. Several times in the book of Acts, people spoke in tongues and saw visions. So why do so many "People of the Book" get defensive about things of the Spirit?

What I have come to understand is that some people truly identify with the Bible because they can see the words of the page, and they strive to live out what is taught. The Word is true; it should be the foundation. Other people identify with their experiences. They have had times where things happened in their lives which were unexplainable, other than to say God did a great work. After they have experienced the living power of God, mere traditional rhetoric will not suffice. They want and seek after a fresh moving of the Spirit.

On one hand, those who identify with the empirical written Word of God tend to view *experience* as a potential gateway for deception. How do we know what people call speaking in tongues isn't just the babbling of an emotional show? How do we know it isn't Satan bringing in confusion and chaos? Besides, there have been so many fraudulent "faith healers" who have conned hurting people out of a lot of money. Also, where is the proof? How do we know that the person who had a supposed "out of body experience" after a car accident really went to Heaven? To those who rely on the black and white letter of Scripture, the charismatic moving of the Spirit is dangerous and disorderly. Not to mention, the testimonies of the Spirit's teachings and movings, while inspiring, are not verifiable. We cannot control the accuracy of those testimonies; that's why many would think they are best left out of the worship service.

Yet for those who long for the power-filled moving of the Holy Spirit of God, nothing could be more powerless than to just know about someone but never experience them. What good is it to know of the three missionary journeys of Paul if you do not experience the God Who called Him on the Damascus Road? Why would God have the New Testament writers list spiritual gifts such as mercy, giving, teaching, and shepherding alongside gifts like tongues, interpretation of tongues, and prophecy if they were not all to be used? Besides, who wants to be a part of a congregation that sings "Joy to the World" with a frown on their face? Worship should use the emotions God gave us. Those in this camp would likely say we do not need to control or prove the Spirit's work because the Spirit will do that Himself; therefore, our testimonies are just as important in worship as the reading of the Word.

Sadly, we have taken things of the Spirit and separated them from the things of Truth, and we have formed congregations around each which we call churches. This division is drawn on the lines of what the Bible says versus what the Bible talks about. But God is not looking for worshippers who will worship Him in spirit *or* truth but, instead, those who worship in spirit *and* truth. This is not something you can just read about in a book but, rather, something God must walk you through. "God is spirit" (John 4:24); and the Spirit blows like the wind, coming and going. Those who are born of the Spirit must be willing to blow like the wind, too. This requires a letting go of control. So many churches today are run by pastors and committees with an iron grip trying to hold the control of the church so that the wind won't blow anything down. Their grip is so tight that the church resembles them more than it does the Body of Christ. But likewise, other congregations have released control and extended open arms to any wonderful thing that comes down the pipe. The issue is that Satan masquerades like an angel of light (II Cor. 11:14). If a church operates on the premise, "If it moves you, embrace it," then we will find ourselves cuddled up with the devil.

Joining the Walls

God did not call the Church to know everything about Him, but we are called to know Him. He desires for us to experience His presence and not for us to be blind nitwits who do not know the difference between light and dark, truth and lies, or God-worship and self-worship. We are to worship Him "in spirit and truth." You cannot experience a truth; you have to know truth. You are not called to just know about the Spirit; you are to walk with the Spirit. Together, walking with the Spirit in the knowledge of the truth is a worship unknown in the ranks of most churches today. Truth be told, it is something most congregations fear.

It is understandable that you will more easily identify with either the empirical Word or the leading Spirit, but Jesus is the Cornerstone of these walls. It is within these walls that we worship the God of Heaven. And it is within this spiritual house that truth can be revealed. The Holy Spirit of God is alive; and He desires to teach us, equip us, lead us, empower us, council us, protect us, and reveal truth to us. But we will not draw on this from a book. No, we can only be taught the discipline of spirit-truth worship from God.

Spirit-Truth Worship

What does spirit-truth worship look like? Let's look at a very popular verse of Scripture, Act 1:8: "'But you will receive power when the Holy Spirit has come upon you; and you shall be My witnesses both in Jerusalem, and in all Judea and Samaria, and even to the remotest part of the earth." This verse is utilized when encouraging people to get out and share the Gospel, but there are a couple things I want us to notice.

First, this verse is not the beginning of a sentence. The sentence begins in verse seven, and the thought begins in verse six. In context, Jesus has gathered all of His followers together; and they are asking Him if the time has come for Him to set up His kingdom (v. 6). He responds by telling them it's not their business to know the times of events God has fixed in place (v. 7).

Then, Jesus continues that sentence with verse eight. Therefore, before you can be a witness through the power of the Holy Spirit, you must surrender to His sovereignty over you. God knows the times; He knows what the plan is; He knows the heart of those lost; and He knows our hearts as well. We must surrender our good ideas for His God sovereignty. We will not figure His plan out on our own. We must seek Him if we are to know His desire.

Finally, it is vitally important to understand the word used in verse eight for "witness" is not a verb, as if we are to go do something; it is a noun, signifying this is something we are. We are a witness—not because we have done something but because He has done it, and we saw it take place. This does not mean that we have no role to play in the gospel; but instead, our role begins when God gives us marching orders and calls us to begin. We must wait for the Spirit to reveal the game plan; then we must wait for Him to empower us, and then we must wait for Him to say, "Now it is time to move forward." That is spirit-truth worship, which is pleasing to the Father. We must wait with our spirit ears straining to hear the call of God and then move in the power that comes from Him.

The Bible formulates it this way in Romans 11:36, "For from Him and through Him and to Him are all things. To Him be the glory forever. Amen." It is not important how much we know, how strong we are, or how good we are. What is important is our willingness to wait for the Spirit's revealing and His empowering and whether we will give the glory back to Him. This cannot be done haphazardly. We must test the Spirit's moving and check everything against the Word of God.

The Lure

If a church was a boat, most pastors would want to make sure it does not rock too much. One congregation will focus on knowing the Bible, and they will talk about the Spirit as long as it does not rock the boat. They don't want to allow too much uncertainty because that would be disorderly. It's not that they don't believe in the Spirit or His movings, but they just focus on what they can see and understand. Other congregations will seek the power of the Spirit while they quote Scripture, which coincides with what they are feeling inside; but they are not as interested in deep Bible study because they want a fresh word.

People do not like it when the boat starts to rock, but it is important to note that Jesus called Peter to get out of the boat. As long as we are looking to see if the boat is rocking, then our eyes can't be on the Savior Who is walking on the water. This is when we start to sink. Then we cling to the boat and vow never to get too far from safety again. I pray that we will learn to forget about the needless boat and its fearful rocking. May we learn that in God's presence, we can worship Him "in spirit and truth." He is the Cornerstone which holds the walls together. May He be glorified as He builds us into His house of worship.

O Cornerstone,
You alone connect the walls of Spirit and Truth.
I am a living stone chosen by Your nail-pierced hands
to be built up into a spiritual house of worship to the Father.
May I never neglect the part of You I do not understand
for the part of You I've become comfortable with.
May the despised Gentile also know their place in Your family.

KNOWING THE FATHER

Ralph looked out the window at his son, Thomas, playing basketball in the backyard. Thomas would soon be sixteen years old, and Ralph was saddened at the fact that he barely knew his son. He got up from his chair and walked outside to Thomas.

"Hey, bud, let's play some ball."

Thomas looked oddly at his dad and said, "That's okay, Dad; I'm tired." Then he walked into the house and closed the door to his room.

Ralph's heart sank even lower as he thought about all those years he missed being "dad" while working overtime in a garage and was absent from doing things with his son. He shrugged and started to walk back to his chair when suddenly it hit him. "All my years in an auto garage could be the very thing that will bring my son back to me." With that, Ralph began brainstorming an idea to start a new relationship with his son.

Finally, the day came. Ralph was so nervous that he couldn't stand it. He knew his crazy idea would not be well-received at first by Thomas; but if they were going to start again, he had to go to the bottom and work his way up. Thomas stumbled out of his bedroom with his hair going everywhere and his eyes barely open. Ralph noted that Thomas looked a foot taller since he started cooking up this plan. Today was his sixteenth birthday, but he looked more like a man.

"Happy Birthday, bud!" Ralph said loudly.

Thomas just kept walking to the bathroom.

As the father and son sat around a breakfast table, Ralph leaned in and told Thomas, "Hey, bud, I got a little something for your birthday out in the driveway."

Thomas' head shot up; and with great excitement, he jumped out of his chair exclaiming, "You got me a car?"

Ralph just grinned and said, "Go look in the driveway."

Thomas ran out the door and around the corner of the house. By the time Ralph got there, Thomas had a bewildered look on his face. In the driveway were several crates and boxes, but not a car. Thomas looked at his dad for an explanation.

"Several months ago, I realized you were about to turn sixteen and would want a car. I knew you had always loved Mustangs, so I searched everywhere and finally found all the parts needed to build a 1965 Shelby GT350."

Thomas looked more confused than ever; and as he processed what his dad had said, the look of disappointment raced across his face. Ralph knew this wasn't what his son wanted; he wanted a car to drive, not one to build. But he also knew if his son had a car, he would drive out of his life forever. Ralph's hope was that they could build their relationship together as they built the car. As the house door slammed behind his son, Ralph was left with stacks of crates and boxes.

Days passed, and Ralph spent each evening in the garage tinkering on the car. Each day, he would ask Thomas if he wanted to help; but each time, Thomas would roll his eyes and walk off.

One evening, Thomas looked into the garage at his dad, whose hands were black with grease while sweat was rolling off his head. "Dad," he said, "I don't know how to build a car."

Ralph looked up. "I know, but I do; and I'll help you."

Begrudgingly, Thomas walked into the garage and looked at the random parts and piles of car everywhere. "What do I do first?" asked Thomas, and that is where the healing began.

It took the better part of a year for Ralph and Thomas to build the car. Night after night, weekend after weekend, they worked diligently on the car; and when it was finished, Thomas was the proud owner of a shiny, red 1965 Shelby GTO350 Mustang, which would make him the envy of his school.

When the morning came for him to make his maiden voyage to school in his new car, Thomas said he felt sick and stayed in bed. Ralph walked into Thomas' room knowing his plan was still not complete. "What's the matter, bud?" he asked.

Thomas and his dad had done a lot of talking during all those late nights in the garage, so he rolled over in bed and said, "Dad, I don't know how to drive a stick shift. Everyone is going to laugh at me when I stall out." Thomas had learned to drive in the family minivan, but he had no idea how to drive a manual. The car would be the envy of the school, but Thomas would be the laughingstock.

"Son, I have an idea. What if you skip school today, and we take your car out for a test run? I know how to drive a stick shift, and I'll help you."

That day was the greatest day of Ralph's life. He and Thomas drove for hours from one end of the state to the other. They listened to music, ate greasy diner food, and laughed every time Thomas stalled out. That night, the Mustang was put to rest in the garage; and Ralph and Thomas turned out the light and walked inside.

Ralph was heading for his chair when he heard Thomas clear his throat. He looked back at his son, whose head was down. "Dad," he said, "I just wanted to say thank you."

Ralph's plan was complete; he had bridged the gap between him and his son. "You're welcome, bud. I love you."

The next day, Thomas drove his car to school; and everyone drooled with envy. When Ralph got home from work that afternoon, Thomas met him at the door. "Dad, there's a car show this weekend, and I was wondering if I could go?"

Ralph thought about it for a moment and then said, "Have fun."

Thomas then added, "The issue is, I don't know how to get there; but I figured you do. Would you like to go with me?"

Ralph now understood more than ever the value of those crates and boxes that had sat in his driveway. His son loved him; but what's more, he wanted to spend time with his dad.

Father of Lights

"Every good thing given and every perfect gift is from above, coming down from the Father of lights, with whom there is no variation or shifting shadow" (James 1:17). What is it that the Father of lights gives? What impact does His gifts have on our lives? We know He gave His Son, thereby giving salvation (John 3:16). The impact of that gift soars past this life and throughout all eternity. The Father of lights gives His Spirit to those who ask for it (Luke 11:13). The Holy Spirit is what brings eternity into our finite lives. God gives us everything we need for life and godliness, which turns our days into opportunities of worship (II Peter 1:3). It is so true; the gifts of the Father are good.

Land Flowing with Milk and Honey

Let's take just a moment to crawl down the rabbit hole of God's good gifts. In Exodus 3:17, Moses records, "So I said, I will bring you up out of the affliction of Egypt to the land of the Canaanite and the Hittite and the Amorite and the Perizzite and the Hivite and the Jebusite, to a land flowing with milk and honey." God tells Moses that He is going to give the Children of Israel a land flowing with milk and honey. What does that even mean? Who would want such a sticky mess? We usually think of milk and honey as prosperity, and while that is true, why does it mean that? There are three things that the Father of lights is promising Moses here: land, milk, and honey. Each of these is vital for Israel's life.

First, God promised a land. This is important because God wasn't just promising them "some land, somewhere." The Father was specifically saying it was the land owned and inhabited by the Canaanites, the Hittites, the Amorites, the Perizzites, the Hivites, and the Jebusites. Not all land is considered a good gift. Land that has been contaminated by toxic waste may be land, but no one would want it gifted to them. Likewise, if you want to start a farm, you would not want a plot of land in the middle of the desert. The land that God is promising the Israelites has to be land that can support and sustain a growing nation. There must be resources, such as trees, water, gardens, roads, etc. Someone may gift you a marvelous mansion; but if it doesn't have land to sit on, then the house is not a good gift. So, the Father of lights is giving the children of Israel land which will support them.

Next, God promises to give them a land flowing with milk. This seems really weird, as long as you are envisioning a fresh spring of milk bubbling out of the ground or a stream of milk flowing through the mountains. But this is not how God designed milk to flow. Milk comes from cows and goats, which means that if God is promising that milk will flow, then the land must come completely equipped with livestock. Yes, God was supplying a land already inhabited with cows and goats. Now, don't stop too quickly here. Cows cannot survive without feed. Therefore, God is also supplying land suitable for enough grazing to sustain enough cows to sustain the needs of the Israelites. Cattle also need water to drink if they are to survive, so this land must have plenty of streams and lakes.

Again, do not stop yet. Cattle are useful for more than just milk. Cows provide leather for clothes, storage, and shelter and also supply meat in abundance. One cow can provide food for many families. Continuing on, a cow cannot produce milk unless it has given birth. So it stands to reason, to have a land flowing with milk, the cows which produce the milk have also provided future generations of cattle. For cows to get pregnant with a calf, there must be a bull somewhere; and bulls are useful for pulling carts and plowing fields for vegetables. The Father of lights is so good.

Finally, God promised a land flowing with milk and honey. What is so good about honey? Honey is a delicious, sweet treat, but it can also be used in cooking and baking to add flavor to meals. Sweetness is not a necessity of life, which means that God is saying that He is also giving the food of joy. The Father did not promise a land flowing with milk and wheat, which would have been practical, but rather, honey, which is a blessing of pleasure. But just like milk, honey doesn't just flow down the sides of mountains; it comes from bees. Bees do not just produce honey from thin air; they have to collect nectar from plants. As the bees collect the nectar, they are also pollinating the plants so that the plants can bear fruit. The plants which were being pollinated could have been flowers of beauty or of crops which were to be eaten. Honey doesn't just mean the Israelites were getting a sweet treat, but they were also getting fruits and vegetables. The cornucopia of life is filled from the work of bees. Not to mention, honey is also a natural antibiotic, which means God was providing for their health as well as their stomachs.

Now, let's put all of the pieces together. When the Father of lights promised Moses that He would give the Israelites a land flowing with milk and honey, they were getting everything they needed: property to live on, sustainable food for generations to come, shelter, resources to work with, clothing, ingredients to cook with, medical help, transportation, healthy foods full of vitamins and minerals, sweet treats, and so much more. This is the God I serve! He is the Giver of all good gifts.

What are some things God has given you and your family that are your "milk and honey?"

_____

_____

_____

I Don't Want That

Have you ever been given something that was on your wish list but was actually slightly off from what you wanted? For example, maybe you asked for some nice quality jewelry. But when you opened the box, the person did, indeed, give you jewelry; but it was a pack of two necklaces, five bracelets, and three rings of a lesser quality. In their mind, they gave you more; but what you were hoping for was quality. This is a case of the giver and receiver not being on the same page.

This is often the case when the Father is the Giver and we are the receiver. Imagine what you would think if God told you He was about to pour out milk and honey on you. There is a good chance we would get an attitude with Him because milk stinks when it spoils and honey attracts flies. How sad it would have been for the Israelites if God had made this promise with them, but they said, "No, thank You." It is vitally important to remember that God understands what we do not; therefore, we need to be grateful for what He gives us because it is exactly what we need.

A great example of this is found in John 14:27: "Peace I leave with you; My peace I give to you; not as the world gives do I give to you. Do not let your heart be troubled, nor let it be fearful." If God came to me and said, "I'm going to give you peace," I would be ecstatic!

But if He followed it up with, "But it's not going to be peace like you think of it," I would begin to wonder what kind of peace it would be. In my understanding, there is only one kind of peace; and that is the absence of fighting. If the peace God is going to give is not the absence of fighting, then what other kind of peace is there? Truth be told, I really like the idea of not fighting anymore; but the thought of being told I have peace while I'm still fighting seems like a cheap gift.

This is how we process the world around us. Christians are quick to think through salvation as if it is a pass to live on "Easy Street." This is why people ask the age-old question, "Why does God allow bad things to happen to good people?" What they are really saying is, "If God is so good and His salvation is complete, then why wouldn't He just take us to Heaven now? Why do we have to wait while living in suffering?" We give very little thought to the fact that if God removed all Christians from the earth at the moment of salvation, then who would share the Good News with a broken world? We have salvation, along with the promise of eternity without pain or death; but what we really want is eternal bliss right now. This is because we do not understand the true gift or the Father Who is the Gift-giver.

Where's My Gift?

It is incredible to think about how God supplied the Israelites with everything they needed; but if we are honest, it's easy to begin questioning God about where my gift is. This is true especially when you read passages like Matthew 7:7-8: "'Ask, and it will be given to you; seek, and you will find; knock, and it will be opened to you. For everyone who asks receives, and he who seeks finds, and to him who knocks it will be opened.'" What are we supposed to do with verses like this? We ask for healings, possessions, jobs, or even hope; but often, we do not get what we asked for.

Before we can go too far in answering that question, we must first submit to the fact that God's ways are higher than ours; so we do not know why God gives to us or withholds from us as He does, but He is righteous either way. Another perspective we need to consider is why we are asking for our request in the first place. Think about it: most of what we ask for in prayer is truly to make us more independent from God. We would not usually phrase it this way; but basically what we are actually saying to God is, "Lord please provide me with what I want so I do not have to keep coming to You for my daily bread."

For most of us, we struggle with only viewing the Father as a spiritual vending machine; and we get upset when He doesn't deliver on our wishes. If God gave us a car, we would likely drive off, leaving Him in our dust. Even Eve, when she ate the fruit in the garden, was trying to gain a wisdom that would make her like God, thereby not needing to go to Him for it. The Father of lights is the Giver of all good gifts but not the giver of all gifts you wish for. What He supplies is good, but what is good? Who makes that determination? Obviously, God knows if it is good; and He makes the judgment call of whether or not to give us what we ask for. But we can rest assured that what God deems good enough to give us is not going to be something that will separate us from His presence. His desire is for us to find our needs met in Him. He is more than enough to supply all we need.

Ephesians 3:20 says, "Now to Him who is able to do far more abundantly beyond all that we ask or think, according to the power that works within us." What does this mean? We understand the first part, where God can do more than we can imagine; but what about the power working in us? The Spirit of God is the power working within us. His presence is greater than any new vehicle, any amount of money, or any new house. We pray for the healing of a family member, but what benefit would that be apart from the presence of God? The Father of lights is not interested in giving us gifts that would separate us from Him; but instead, He wants to whet our appetite with His presence so we want Him even more.

The Lure

The blessing of the gift is not the gift itself but, instead, the love that drove the Gift-giver to give it to you. Our hearts long for so much while we live here on this planet. But so much of what we desire either separates us from the Father or makes us independent of the Father, or the Father has already given it to us in His Word with some assembly required. We may not know the blueprint for true peace, but the Father knows it. We may not know how to assemble courage, but the Father would happily reveal this to us. We may not understand healing that lasts; but the Father wants nothing more than to spend time with us, teach us, and mesmerize our minds with His grandeur.

The Father of lights is the Giver of all good gifts, but we must know the heart of the Giver if we are to appreciate the gift. We can never know the Father's heart unless we abide in His presence, walk with Him, align with Him, and long for His return. What if when we get to Heaven, we learn all we ever asked for was yes in the Spirit; but we spent our whole lives complaining about not having it our way. What if we missed His presence while we cried out to be independent of Him? What if His presence was more than we could ever ask or think or imagine? There is complete provision in His presence.

This lifestyle of gratitude for the Father's gift won't just happen. This is a discipline that will only be learned from walking with the Spirit over a lifetime. How could we appreciate the peace Jesus gives until we walk through a war in the presence of the Father? He will not alleviate the fight, but His presence will teach us that He is good. Yes, He is also greater and capable and awesome; but sometimes, we simply need to learn that the Father is good.

O Father of lights,
Your light shines in the darkness,
and it reveals the cracks in my arrogance.
I think I know better than You,
but I do not understand Your ways.
Please teach me to walk in Your presence.
Lure me into a life of gratitude for Your gifts.
May I know the provision of Your presence.
May I know Your goodness.

WATCHING FOR MESSIAH

Derek awoke to the glare of a very hot sun and the soreness of a body which had been through a great deal. His mind raced as he tried to put the pieces together. Why was he lying face down on a sandy beach? Why was he hurting so badly? Where was he? What happened?

Slowly, memories of fire and screams began to come back to him. He had been a cabin boy on a ship, sailing to the Americas. Derek remembered the crew laughing and the passengers singing on deck. Vaguely, he recalled the sound of glass breaking and looking up to see a kerosine lamp shattered on the deck, having been knocked over by a couple of boys playing around. The fuel caught fire and quickly spread. Passengers screamed, and sailors ran around trying to put the fire out. The fire grew rapidly, and passengers began jumping overboard. Lifeboats were lowered; but before they could get to the water, the flames hit a powder keg. And then everything went white. He did not remember anything after that. Now he was lying face down on a beach alone and surrounded by charred wreckage.

Slowly, Derek got up and checked for injuries. He was very grateful to find he only had cuts and scrapes. He walked around in a daze, looking at the debris on the beach. There was nothing among the wreckage but some torn canvas from the sails, part of a busted suitcase, burned boards, and a glass bottle. The island itself didn't appear to be very large and was fairly flat. Derek was in shock. He couldn't wrap his mind around what was going on. He walked over to a tree and collapsed.

He must have slept for some time because when we woke up, the sun was just rising over the horizon. Today would be a new day, and he would see what he could do to save his life. He found some fruit on some trees and was able to get some water from a coconut. Using some of the pieces of sail, he made a little makeshift covering to rest under. There were no signs of life anywhere on the island or out to sea.

Finally, with a start, Derek jumped up and ran down to the wreckage and grabbed the glass bottle. It was intact and even had a cork in the top of it. It was the perfect vessel to deliver his cry for help. He ripped off a small piece of the sail; and then taking a charred piece of wood from the wreckage, he sat down under a tree and began to think. If this was his only chance of writing for help, what could he say that would draw the finder to him?

Derek thought about his note for the rest of the day; and then finally, with solemn resignation, he wrote:

> *Where I am I do not know,*
> *I cannot tell you where to go.*
> *But if you promise to come for me,*
> *I will always watch where sky meets sea.*

The Sweetest of Days

The sweetest things in life are usually made sweeter by the passing of time before you receive them. We wouldn't really understand the sweetness of the moment unless we knew firsthand the bitterness of the days which had led up to it. There is coming a day which, compared to all moments prior—no matter how sweet they have been and no matter how perfect they appeared—will be the sweetest of all. It will be the sweetest because it has been the most awaited moment in history. We cannot even comprehend the splendor of this moment because it has been anticipated far longer than we have been alive. The only One Who can grasp the magnitude of this event is God Almighty because only He has waited for it from the beginning. The fulfillment of this long-awaited day will be marked as the sweetest because it will be the fulfillment of the purpose of the cross. All the pain, wounds, scars, and silence of the cross will fade away as Jesus steps out of Heaven and calls His brothers and sisters home.

Set in Motion

The day of the first human sin was the day of the first prophecy. God would speak in one sentence of the entirety of the pain throughout humanity, the rise and destruction of all that is evil, the hope of all who would call on His great Name, and the longing of everything eternal in the heavenlies. The prophecy of that day is found in Genesis 3:15: "And I will put enmity Between you and the woman, And between your seed and her seed; He shall bruise you on the head, And you shall bruise him on the heel." God speaks these words as a curse to the serpent, whose twisted words tempted Eve and then Adam into eating the fruit of the tree of knowledge. This curse speaks of a war between good and evil, which would span generations and would come to an end with the destruction of evil and the mortal wounding of the seed of the Good.

From that moment on, humanity has waited for the coming of the seed of the woman who would crush the head of the evil serpent. While yes, we have anticipated justice and judgment to be served on Satan, we are also longing for the restoration of our relationship with the Father. These are the two sides of the coin of life. One side is that of justice and judgment poured out on the sin of the world, and the other side is the restored relationship with God. Let's crack this open because the truth that lies in the center of it is the very truth which will lure us into God's presence.

Justice and Judgment

How glorious the day will be when Satan is finally crushed. But what does this actually mean? We quickly show our approval at the prophecies of his demise in the Lake of Fire. We would even volunteer to be a member of his firing squad. But in so aligning ourselves with the destruction of Satan for his lies, hate, and death, we condemn ourselves to the same fate. This may have been Satan's craftiest plot against the Father. In losing his own life, he also condemns to Hell the very thing God longs for. An eternity of Hell for Satan is to be an eternity of separation for God from His precious creation. This is justice; this is judgment. To crush the serpent's head is to crush God's heart.

Yet the Good News of the Gospel is that while we were still dying in disobedience and destruction, Christ surrendered His life in exchange for our death (Rom. 5:8). This was the judgment and justice meant for us, which was poured out on Jesus instead. The full blow that Satan received for his rebellion also hit Jesus on the cross.

Our Relationship with God

The other side of this coin is having been forgiven for our sin, we desire to have a restored relationship with the Father. God walked in the Garden of Eden with Adam and Eve in the cool of the day (Gen. 3:8). He walked with humanity. There was no separation. It was a union which we cannot comprehend because we have never known it. His presence is not like that of the presence of a wife or husband; but instead, walking in the presence of God is to walk in life itself. We have never known life to this level because of the death which clings to us. To walk with God as Adam walked with God is to know no death. Yet as God's grace washes our wretched filth away, we begin to see the awe-inspiring presence of God; and we desire to live in His presence unhindered by our limited finite bodies. That day has not come yet. As Paul states in I Corinthians 13:12, "For now we see in a mirror dimly, but then face to face; now I know in part, but then I will know fully just as I also have been fully known."

Truth be told, a single glimpse of a dim reflection of God's glory is greater than a clear view of all the glories of this earth for an eternity. Nothing of death can compare to life. But to eyes that have grown accustomed to the dark, light can be repulsive. Eyes which have been focused on the things of this world lose their longing for God's presence, and they must be lured back. But rest assured, that day of restoration is coming like an unexpected shooting star. For the one who tires of watching the night sky, they will miss the majesty of the heavens coming to earth.

A Returning Christ

If we are to grasp the wonder of being restored to God's presence, then we must appreciate John 14:2-3: "In My Father's house are many dwelling places; if it were not so, I would have told you; for I go to prepare a place for you. If I go and prepare a place for you, I will come again and receive you to Myself, that where I am, *there* you may be also." Jesus said He was going to leave for a time so that He could prepare a place for us, but he would be coming back. Do you really believe that one day, Jesus will return to take us home; or do you just think this was some metaphor for something? This is very important because if He is coming back, then we had better be ready.

Watching the Horizon

> "Be dressed in readiness, and *keep* your lamps lit. Be like men who are waiting for their master when he returns from the wedding feast, so that they may immediately open *the door* to him when he comes and knocks. Blessed are those slaves whom the master will find on the alert when he comes; truly I say to you, that he will gird himself *to serve*, and have them recline *at the table*, and will come up and wait on them. Whether he comes in the second watch, or even in the third, and finds *them* so, blessed are those *slaves*" (Luke 12:35-38).

> "Who then is the faithful and sensible slave whom his master put in charge of his household to give them their food at the proper time? Blessed is that slave whom his master finds so doing when he comes. Truly I say to you that he will

put him in charge of all his possessions. But if that evil slave says in his heart, 'My master is not coming for a long time,' and begins to beat his fellow slaves and eat and drink with drunkards; the master of that slave will come on a day when he does not expect *him* and at an hour which he does not know, and will cut him in pieces and assign him a place with the hypocrites; in that place there will be weeping and gnashing of teeth" (Matt. 24:45-51).

Jesus came to this earth as a little baby, and then He grew up and ministered for three years. He would lay down His life and then pick it back up again before ascending back to His home in Heaven to prepare a place for us. But He would leave us with these instructions, "I'm coming back to get you, so be ready." His return could be at any moment of any day of any week of any year. How could we possibly stand constantly ready, unless we devoted our entire life to His reappearing? But that is the difference between the blessed and cursed slave Jesus told us about.

In Luke 12:35-36, Jesus told us about a slave who was given a job when his master left for a wedding. The master told him to simply watch the horizon so that when he got back home, the door would be opened for him. The master wanted the slave to remain ready. Certainly, it would not be an easy assignment to stay watchful day and night until the master returned, but the slave desired something more than his own lusts. He desired the great pleasure of the master. He desired the presence of the master. As soon as the slave saw the master's chariot come over the horizon, the slave would smile and open the door wide because he knew that soon the master would bring him into the house and would spend time with him. For this slave, the wait was nothing compared to the presence of the master.

Next, in Matthew 24:42-51, the master gave the slave a different task. He was to take care of the master's household by making sure they were given food at the proper time. The master trusted this slave to take care of everything from the time he would leave until he returned. But this slave grew tired of watching the horizon day after day. He lost sight of the good pleasure of his master. Now disillusioned, this slave would leave his post and would begin to live for himself. Not only did he not pass food out to the household, but he also stole from his master's table. That which the master had provided for his household was then used for revelry with those outside the master's house.

But this slave was caught off guard when his master came home and found those in the master's care were hungry and in need. Those who are in the charge of the master do not go in need. But here they are lacking, and that which the master intended for their care has been squandered by those outside the house. This slave stands without excuse because he was not watching the horizon. His rebuke would not be a slap on the wrist. Nor would it be to go to the back of the line. He would lose the presence of his master. He would be assigned to a place the master never treads. His momentary pleasures would cost him the opportunity to walk with his master. How sad.

The Master's Return

Truly, the day is coming when our Master will return. We have been charged to watch the horizon for that day. He has been preparing a place for us, and He has asked us to feed those of His household until

He returns. How are you doing? Do you still stand at your post? Is your shirt clean and pressed so that when the master returns, He will find you representing Him well? Have you grown weary of watching the eastern sky? Has your soul begun to doubt His promise to return? Even worse, have you begun dipping into the Master's resources and partying with those outside His house? Wake up, dreamer! A lifetime of waiting here is but a fleeting moment in eternity. Do not trade His presence for trinkets of fool's gold. Remember what the Master gave up so that He could walk with you. Your judgment and justice were served in full on the Master's Son so that upon His return, we would be able to walk with Him as one who has never known death.

What do you believe the Master has called you to do while He is away? If you do not know, then how can you find out? Are you living these things out? Ask Him to reveal His desires to you.

The Lure

The sweetest of all days is still to come. The longer we wait for the return of the Messiah, the sweeter that day will be. The prophecy was given at the beginning: the seed of the woman would crush the head of the serpent. This would cost the Messiah dearly because pouring judgment on the serpent would be pouring judgment on us as well. That is justice. In order for us to walk with the Father, the Son took our judgment on Himself—His robe of Life in exchange for our rags of death. Now we have something pleasing to wear when the Messiah returns.

May His robe of righteousness still linger with the scent of our Master. May His scent fill our nostrils daily so that we will not grow weary of watching the horizon. May we long for that coming day when Jesus crests the eastern sky and we soar to meet Him in the clouds. We know that the Father will greet us with open arms; and we will walk with Him and see Him, not dimly as in a mirror but face to face. He goes to prepare a place for us. He will return just like He said He would. While awaiting for His return, make sure the household of God is fed and that the hinges on the gate to the Master's house do not squeak and fix your eyes toward Heaven. His presence awaits.

Oh, Messiah,
My heart longs to see You rightly.
I shiver with anticipation of Your return.
May Your Spirit awaken me so that I do not
fall asleep during the task at hand.
Trinkets from this world sparkle all around me,
but may I not be enticed to steal from You to give to Satan.
May I stand ready with the hope that one day You will return;
and on that day, we will celebrate together,
walking hand in hand.

TRUSTING THE SUNRISE FROM ON HIGH

"Dark Night & Joyful Morning"

Back and forth, up and down,
Like a ship tossed by a stormy sea.
My mind races and searches for a happy place.
Yet every island of joy is marred by the images in my head.

I seek a peace to this storm,
But the waves keep raging.
"Help!" I cry. "I need Your help, Lord."
"Aren't You the One Who calms the storm?"

Run, run, run. My mind is running from itself.
I'm my biggest enemy right now.
My mind betrays me,
But it can't help it. It's scared.

Lord, please pick me up and hold me tight
Like a little baby in Your arms.
My eyes grow weary, and they want to close.
May I lay my head on Your shoulder and rest awhile.

I'm so tired, yet my eyes are afraid to close.
What lies in the dark is unknown, yet feared.
Lack of faith in You, Lord? I pray not.
For my faith in You is all I've got.

Hold my hand and help me rest.
Give me strength to sleep.
This night is long but part of the journey.
Tomorrow is a new day, and joy will come in the morning.

The Uncertainty of Darkness

Have you ever walked in pitch black darkness? It is so disconcerting. Your toes have a way of just about curling under your foot to keep from getting stumped. It is as if the shadows, which do not even exist, seem to shift and move. And the strange noises we hear in the night always seem to sound louder in the dark. Darkness plays all kinds of tricks on us. But that is not exactly true. When you walk in the light, you are able to walk with confidence and surety of step; but in the dark, you have uncertainty with you.

Uncertainty breeds anxiety, and anxiety breeds fear. Fear is an emotion that keeps us safe, but it is also an emotion we are to control through the power of the Holy Spirit. Fear that is out of control drifts from protecting us to destroying us. The perfect love God has for us will cast out our fear (I John 4:18), but we must walk in His love. Now, let's put the pieces together. Walking in the dark produces fear, but walking in the love of God casts out fear. So what happens when God leads you into darkness? The psalmist says, "Even though I walk through the valley of the shadow of death, I fear no evil, for You are with me" (Psalm 23:4). There are times when God leads us through shadows of darkness and uncertainty. How are we to walk in the light of His love and not the shadow of fear?

Fear

Before we get to the light of God, let's examine the fear of darkness. What is fear? Everyone has experienced it to some extent. Nightmares can wake us up in a cold sweat; walking down a dark street causes us to look over our shoulder; and if you have ever had your children get out of your sight in a store, then you know what it is to fear the possibilities.

Simply put, fear is "the expectation of bad." We look at a situation and assess it; and then if the scenario that ranks top for probability has a "bad" or negative outcome, fear is the emotion that takes center stage. The issue is we are trying to assess a future event based on limited present information and past experience, often to the exclusion of supernatural intervention; and we arrive to the conclusion that we are not enough to control the situation. Our flesh has a draw to the negative, and the negative produces fear in us.

Hope

If fear is the expectation of bad, then hope is the opposite. Hope is the expectation of good. Another way of saying all of this is fear is expecting Satan to move and God to remain still, and hope is the expectation that God is going to move with greater ability than Satan's authority.

When we look at a situation and see we are not adequate to handle it on our own, we have to make a determination about the character of God. Either He is negligent and passive, or He is responsive and good. Your decision concerning God's character will determine which emotion will take control of you.

Hope is a wonderful emotion. Many children will wake up on Christmas morning with the hope of receiving their wish because they believe Santa is good. Many young adults will go on a date with the hope of finding their true love because they believe that person to be good. Many parents will hope their children make it to the big leagues because they are good athletes. But we look at our circumstances with fear because we haven't determined in our own mind that God is good.

God on Trial

Let's be honest, does God's track record show that He is good? He created a beautiful, wonderful, sustainable world. He created humanity in His image. He gave man a woman as a helper. But He also allowed evil to be in the garden with them. He didn't stop Eve from eating the fruit, even though He could have. God did remove humanity from the garden so they couldn't eat from the tree of life and then live forever in their fallen state, yet He did allow mankind to sink further and further into sin until even He was willing to annihilate them in a flood.

But He didn't turn His back on humanity. He saved Noah and his family so they could start over. In time, He chose a people and made a covenant with them. He even provided food for them through Joseph when there was a drought. There again, He allowed them to be enslaved for many years and go through lots of pain. God did finally respond to their slavery with freedom through the Passover, but He disciplined them with forty years of wandering in the wilderness. He graciously gave them a promised land flowing with milk and honey; but He didn't wipe out the enemy, so there was always war.

He brought about a lot of positives in the Jewish nation, but He also allowed a lot of negatives. No wonder the Jewish people wanted a king who could lead them. But God allowed their kings to be corrupt and evil. Sure, there was David, who was a man after God's own heart, except for the whole thing with Bathsheba and Uriah. He allowed His people to be overtaken and even exiled into a pagan land, but He did provide them with prophets who would speak for God. Most of their messages were very harsh words, though. Yet in the end, He brought them back to Israel.

Of course, they would be overtaken by the Romans. But who can forget God loved us enough to send us His only Son so we could have eternal life, though He allowed Jesus to die in order to give that to us? But Jesus rose from the dead. Yet after all that, Jesus left us; but then again, God did send His Spirit to dwell with us. Life has been full of war, murder, greed, cancer, famine, hate, affairs, homelessness, theft, holocausts, slavery, abductions, and death; but there has also been love, families, generosity, awakenings, abolitions, churches, revivals, random acts of kindness, deliverance, medical advances, and life.

With all this evidence on the table concerning the character of God, would you find Him good, bad, or inconclusive? The word that comes out of your mouth can be very different than the emotion that rules your heart. Is your life consumed with fear or with hope? What do you expect God to do? I do not believe you can move forward in life until you settle this.

A Difficult Verse

The goodness of God was something I wrestled with for several years. How can God be good if there is so much bad? In my search for answers to the goodness of God, I came across a verse of Scripture that became a struggle point for me. It is found in Ephesians 6:10: "Finally, be strong in the Lord and in the strength of His might." The Greek word for "might" is *ischys*, which literally means "ability." I am to be strong in the Lord and the strength of His ability. I found this verse while I was struggling with anxiety and panic attacks. From the depths of my heart, I believed in the healing power, deliverance power, and restorative power of God. I trusted in the ability of God to do what I could not do myself; but when He did not take away the anxious fear in my heart, I struggled to trust in the goodness of God.

How can you be strong in the Lord's ability if you cannot trust His willingness to use that ability on His children? Where is the goodness of God if all you can see is the pain? If all you can see is the pain, then all you will experience is the pain. The author of Hebrews said it best: "Fixing our eyes on Jesus, the author and perfecter of faith, who for the joy set before Him endured the cross, despising the shame, and has sat down at the right hand of the throne of God" (Heb. 12:2). We are told to fix our eyes on Jesus not the pain or the circumstances. Jesus understands pain; He endured the cross and the shame. We are to fix our eyes on Him because He is "the author and perfecter of faith." Faith is going to be the key to the goodness of God.

Peace

How do we find peace in the goodness of God when He doesn't utilize His ability to our liking? Faith is the moment we say, "I may not be able to see what You are doing, but I surrender to Your hidden ways, Lord." Once we begin to walk in that faith, we find there is peace in the surrender. For me, I had to come to a point where I said, "I wish I didn't struggle with anxiety, and I know God could stop this if He wanted; but because I am still struggling, there must be a reason beyond my current understanding."

With that said, I do not accept the anxiety, but I do accept the battle. I will daily rise up under the authority of God and proclaim Scripture against anxiety because God, in His goodness, has given me armor and weapons to fight against it. I may not see God's goodness, but I have faith that He is good; and it is through the faith He is writing in me that I can rest in His peace. God's presence in my life does not remove all of life's pain, but it assures me that in the shadows of this life, He is working things for good (Rom. 8:28).

When was a time in your life that darkness seemed to overpower the Light? LORD, I pray that as this reader tells of a dark day, that the Sunrise from on High would rise and illuminate their darkness and shed healing love on their wounds.

A Light in the Darkness

Oftentimes, life is shrouded in darkness. Fear is easier to come by in the darkness than hope, but our faith holds us steady until light breaks through. I vividly remember the day I was mowing the grass at a church. I had spent hours push mowing the endless grass. As I was finishing up, the owner of the property came over and asked about a truck that had been sitting in the parking lot. I had noticed the silhouette of the driver from a distance, but I had tried not to make eye contact as I mowed up against the truck. I told the property owner that I didn't know who it was, but they had been there for a while.

He simply said, "Well, let's go find out."

We walked over to the truck. When we were about ten feet away, we realized, to our horror, that the man had committed suicide. I went into shock. My mind raced, but my body was numb. The police were called, and reports were made. Finally, I went home and waited outside until my family came home. I was scared of my thoughts because the images in my mind terrorized me. The sun went down, and I was left in a very dark night. It was dark outside, but it was also very dark inside me.

My faith was rattled because I could not see the goodness of God. That night seemed to last forever. But finally, the sun crested the horizon; and a new day started. I was still full of fear; but as the days and weeks rolled by, hope began to emerge. My hope was rooted in a faith that God was good, but I just couldn't see it yet. Finally, faith gave way to peace, and peace allowed my soul to rest. I was learning to trust God in the darkness. See, darkness lends itself to fear, which is the expectation of bad. But faith in God's goodness teaches us to trust Him in the darkness so that we can expect good to emerge. We learn to hope for the sun to rise, shedding light into our darkness. We may not have the answers nor the desired outcome, but we can have peace because God is good.

(I wrote the poem at the beginning of this chapter during that long dark night waiting for the sun to rise.)

We do not always see God's hand leading us out of the valley of the shadow of death; but sometimes, the Sunrise from on high reveals Himself so clearly. Fifteen years after that death filled day, I unexpectedly got to see the Son rise with life in His wake. I had been asked by my pastor to help give communion to an elderly church member who was in a nursing home. Without giving it much thought, I agreed.

About the time we arrived at the nursing home, I made the connection; the lady we were going to meet was the widow of the man I had found. Not only that, but his daughter was also in the nursing home. Both wife and daughter were ailing, and even the daughter was confined to bed without the ability to feed herself. When it came time to give the communion elements, I realized that I was going to have to physically put the bread into the daughter's mouth as well as put the cup to her lips. This was the moment death met life, dark met light, fear met forgiveness, and sorrow met joy. Nothing could be further from God's heart than suicide, the ending of the life He gave because of hopelessness. But nothing could be closer to His heart than the love of Jesus flowing from the cross into the lips of those hurting. I was not worthy to be the vessel used by

God to deliver these elements, but I praise God that the Sunrise from on high crested the horizon of my life at that moment with healing and hope in its midst. Praise God!

> "Because of the tender mercy of our God, With which the Sunrise from on high will visit us, TO SHINE UPON THOSE WHO SIT IN DARKNESS AND THE SHADOW OF DEATH, To guide our feet into the way of peace" (Luke 1:78-79).

The Lure

Eyes that have grown accustomed to the dark squint when a light is turned on. Likewise, a life that embraces the dark shutters when the light of Christ exposes it. The light hurts our eyes, and it brings shame to our way of life; but oh, the freedom that comes to those who walk in the Light. How can we possibly know the heart of God while stumbling in the dark? Those who stumble in the dark curse God for His cruelty. But those who walk in His light praise Him, for they no longer have to fear. The perfect love of the Father has cast out their fear. Can you imagine living life out of the shadows, free to walk in the light as He is in the light, and to walk with the Father, hand in hand, as the Sunrise from on high announces a new day?

Oh, Sunrise from on high,
Greater are Your ways than I can understand.
Please teach us to hope because if we cannot trust in Your goodness,
then all we have left is fear. May we trust in Your goodness,

even when we cannot see because of the darkness. May faith hold us through the night until You rise above the horizon, and then we will know Your goodness fully.

WONDERLURE

My prayer for you is that you will walk with Emmanuel, follow the Lamb, abide on the Vine, align with the Cornerstone, know the Father, watch for the Messiah, and trust the Sunrise from on high. Now, may you meditate on His Word and allow Him to lure you into the wonder of His presence.

- **Psalm 97:6:** "The heavens declare His righteousness, And all the peoples have seen His glory."
- **Romans 1:20:** "For since the creation of the world His invisible attributes, His eternal power and divine nature, have been clearly seen, being understood through what has been made, so that they are without excuse."
- **John 1:14:** "And the Word became flesh, and dwelt among us, and we saw His glory, glory as of the only begotten from the Father, full of grace and truth."
- **Psalm 9:10:** "And those who know Your name will put their trust in You, For You, O LORD, have not forsaken those who seek You."

- **Psalm 9:16:** "The LORD has made Himself known; He has executed judgment. In the work of his own hands the wicked is snared."
- **John 10:10:** "The thief comes only to steal and kill and destroy; I came that they may have life, and have it abundantly."
- **John 17:3:** "This is eternal life, that they may know You, the only true God, and Jesus Christ whom You have sent."
- **John 12:32:** "And I, if I am lifted up from the earth, will draw all men to Myself."
- **Jeremiah 29:13:** "You will seek Me and find *Me* when you search for Me with all your heart."
- **Psalm 15:1:** "O LORD, who may abide in Your tent? Who may dwell on Your holy hill?"
- **John 15:5:** "I am the vine, you are the branches; he who abides in Me and I in him, he bears much fruit, for apart from Me you can do nothing."
- **Jeremiah 6:16:** "Thus says the LORD, "Stand by the ways and see and ask for the ancient paths, Where the good way is, and walk in it; And you will find rest for your souls. But they said, *'We will not walk in it.'*"
- **Amos 3:3:** "Do two men walk together unless they have made an appointment?"
- **Matthew 7:22-23:** "Many will say to Me on that day, 'Lord, Lord, did we not prophesy in Your name, and in Your name cast out demons, and in Your name perform many miracles?' And then I will declare to them, 'I never knew you; DEPART FROM ME, YOU WHO PRACTICE LAWLESSNESS.'"

- **II Corinthians 6:16:** "Or what agreement has the temple of God with idols? For we are the temple of the living God; just as God said, "I WILL DWELL IN THEM AND WALK AMONG THEM; AND I WILL BE THEIR GOD, AND THEY SHALL BE MY PEOPLE."
- **Deuteronomy 23:14:** "Since the LORD your God walks in the midst of your camp to deliver you and to defeat your enemies before you, therefore your camp must be holy; and He must not see anything indecent among you or He will turn away from you."
- **I Corinthians 5:7:** "Clean out the old leaven so that you may be a new lump, just as you are *in fact* unleavened. For Christ our Passover also has been sacrificed."
- **Revelation 21:3-7:** "And I heard a loud voice from the throne, saying, 'Behold, the tabernacle of God is among men, and He will dwell among them, and they shall be His people, and God Himself will be among them, and He will wipe away every tear from their eyes; and there will no longer be *any* death; there will no longer be *any* mourning, or crying, or pain; the first things have passed away.' And He who sits on the throne said, 'Behold, I am making all things new.' And He said, 'Write, for these words are faithful and true.' Then He said to me, 'It is done. I am the Alpha and the Omega, the beginning and the end. I will give to the one who thirsts from the spring of the water of life without cost. He who overcomes will inherit these things, and I will be his God and he will be My son.'"
- **Revelation 22:20-21:** "He who testifies to these things says, 'Yes, I am coming quickly.' Amen. Come, Lord Jesus. The grace of the Lord Jesus be with all. Amen."

Take a moment before you close this book and write a prayer to God—not the god you can imagine, nor the god you can put in your neat, clean religious box. Write a prayer to Emmanuel, Who will never leave you; the Lamb of God, Who takes away your sins; the True Vine, which grows joy, peace, and love in you; the Cornerstone that lays the line of truth; the Father, Who is so proud of you; the Messiah Who can't wait to come back and take you home; and the Sunrise, Who sees through your darkness and makes it light! Write a prayer to God and tell Him your struggles, praise Him for His power, and love on Him because He loves you. Allow Him to lure you into the wonder of His presence! May you be blessed as you walk with Him.

ABOUT THE AUTHOR

Jason Lawson lives in North Carolina with his wife, Lindsey, and their three kids, Oliver, Amos, and Salem. Together, they love playing outdoors and experiencing nature. As a family and discipleship pastor, he is passionate about training people of all ages and backgrounds to walk daily with God. Jason has also written *The Potter's Hands*, a 366-day devotional about knowing Who God is.

Check out
www.jasonlawsonbooks.com
www.jasonlawsonbooks.org
FaceBook: Jason Lawson or jasonlawsonbooks
to learn more about what God is doing in Jason's life.

Ambassador International's mission is to magnify the Lord Jesus Christ and promote His Gospel through the written word.

We believe through the publication of Christian literature, Jesus Christ and His Word will be exalted, believers will be strengthened in their walk with Him, and the lost will be directed to Jesus Christ as the only way of salvation.

For more information about AMBASSADOR INTERNATIONAL please visit:

www.ambassador-international.com
@AmbassadorIntl
www.facebook.com/AmbassadorIntl

Thank you for reading this book!

You make it possible for us to fulfill our mission, and we are grateful for your partnership.

To help further our mission, please consider leaving us a review on your social media, favorite retailer's website, Goodreads or Bookbub, or our website, and check out some of the books on the following page!

ALSO AVAILABLE FROM
AMBASSADOR INTERNATIONAL

Finding Hope and Strength in God is a twelve-month devotional with different themes for each month focused on pointing you to your all-sufficient Savior, Who will give you strength and hope to face the day and to live a meaningful and fulfilling Christian life. Its practical approach to life will help you navigate real-life situations with tangible solutions to help you find meaning, hope, strength, and courage despite the tumultuous eventualities of life.

Throughout her years serving alongside her husband, who pastored Southside Baptist Church (now Fellowship Greenville) in Greenville, South Carolina, for over thirty years, Elizabeth Rice Handford has had the opportunity to touch many lives with her daily devotionals. In her new devotional, Fullness of Joy, take a dive into one hundred of Libby's devotionals, compiled from a look back through her writings and life experiences.

www.ingramcontent.com/pod-product-compliance
Lightning Source LLC
Chambersburg PA
CBHW070517100426
42743CB00010B/1846